My
Culinary Academy

By Peter Gebauer

Printed in the United States of America

While the author has made every effort to provide accurate telephone numbers and Internet addresses at the time of publication, neither the publisher nor the author assumes any responsibility for errors, or for changes that occur after publication. Further, the publisher does not have any control over and does not assume any responsibility for author or third-party websites or their content.

ISBN: 1481152831
ISBN-13: 9781481152839

Dedication

For my wife, Aimé, my children Anna Claudia, Daniel and Peter, family, friends, and mentors
Who have been there to support the life of a chef.
I am grateful.

*"What quality is your training program for your cleaners,
cooks, and servers? Is it appropriate and practical
for your operation, and does it address identified
training gaps so that your team at the end of the day
is educated and empowered to deal with your clients
successfully, day in and day out?"*
—Omnivore's Travel

Contents

Acknowledgments

This book was almost ten years in the making and would not have been possible without the support of many; including these dedicated professionals:

Chefs Steve, Robert, Dennis, Tony, Mike, and Mo with their feedback;
Angie Osowski proofreading recipes;
Margaret Regan taking pictures.
Chef Siegfried Schaber and Chef Fritz Sonnenschmidt for their inspiration.
Don Sally, Laurette Pettibone and Mike Goodrich for their support.

Thank you.

My Fujiwara Knives-twenty years in service.

Foreword

In the hotel, resort, and casino food service industry, employee training is a huge operational challenge. Often neglected by owners and managers in favor of room or casino operations, the usual result is job dissatisfaction and high turnover for food and beverage employees. At *Hotel F&B*, it's tough to find real-world hotel training success stories for publication. That's why the Potawatomi Bingo Casino's Culinary Academy—and its accompanying book, *My Culinary Academy*—is a great endeavor, far above what is normally seen in the industry.

I became familiar with the Potawatomi Bingo Casino through the efforts of Executive Chef Peter Gebauer. Over the past decade, Chef Peter has been the source or subject of three magazine feature stories as well as dozens of posts for our internationally circulated *Hotel F&B Observer* online blog. He is also a member of the advisory board for the culinary program at Waukesha County Technical College. How he contributes so much while caring for his young family and full-time job, I do not know. However, we are grateful. It must be said that, since the founding of *Hotel F&B* in 2002, if I had to name one industry professional who had been the most supportive of our editorial mission, Chef Peter would be at the top of my list.

In 2010, Chef Peter said in a blog post introducing the academy: "One of the most vital parts of the culinary-education process is chefs that are dedicated to the educational growth of all team members. From the start of their training, we must ensure that there is a strong support system in the kitchens to enable these young people to rely on their chefs for their educational needs. The chef who trained me once said that the value of being an apprentice is threefold: it is learning, developing relationships, and, most of all, learning how to communicate and work within a community of chefs and cooks."

An apprentice program in the United States is a wonderful thing. Since becoming founding publisher of *Hotel F&B* in 2002, it has intrigued me why the United States—with its gigantic food service industry—doesn't incorporate more European training methods. The obvious answer is cost, but the investment in training can be offset with gains in staff productivity, proficiency, and longevity, not to mention burnishing the overall brand image. Food service positions are valued professional jobs in Europe rather than the temporary or second jobs they often are in America. European cooks, servers, and stewards enter apprentice programs and enjoy lifelong careers. It seems that Chef Peter, a native of Germany, is on to something at the Potawatomi Culinary Academy. We need more of this in the United States.

In 2009, Peter sent me an early draft of *My Culinary Academy*. I'm not culinary trained, but if I were a student, this book would be a cornerstone. It's full of professional fundamentals and challenging end-of-chapter tests on topics ranging from safe knife handling to sushi making to sustainable food sources. Looking at the finished book three years later, I see it has evolved considerably, incorporating all Chef Peter's experience and knowledge. For example, the chapter on wok cookery contains photos of various woks; the history of wok cooking and cooking styles that utilize it; seasoning the wok; cooking methods; safe handling; and specific recipes for wok cookery as featured in Potawatomi's RuYi restaurant. And this is just one chapter.

In June 2010, I traveled to Milwaukee to visit the casino and participate in classes. At the time, I was unaware of the extensive foundation that had been laid down beginning in 2007, when the first class was held with ten students, and moving quickly enough so that, by 2009, several advanced culinary classes were being offered. Chef Peter mischievously placed me in the advanced egg cookery class, where the day's lesson was preparing traditional poached eggs. I struck the egg too hard against the pan, which resulted in a mess. Chef Peter suggested, in his patient way, that I might try a more gentle approach.

I also noted the smart, big-picture perspective from top management down, an emphasis on planning and executing details, and the evident pride of the F&B team members. I felt this everywhere, from the buffet to the Fire Pit and RuYi restaurants and in the back of the house. Particularly in the production kitchen, where I spent some time washing and sorting vegetables, people at all levels in this cold kitchen were energetic, detail oriented, and proud of their good work, their skills, the efficiencies of their work areas, and their food and equipment safety and storage practices. It's a large facility, but there's a feeling of organization and cleanliness. It is always rewarding to visit the front lines in our industry and see it done well.

So now that the academy is hitting full stride and *My Culinary Academy* is on the eve of publication, I realize how persevering and steady Chef Peter has been, meticulously gathering experience and support while tweaking his processes over many years.

Is it working? In an interview with *Shepherd Express*, Chef Peter said, "We are forward thinking and progressive in our curriculum and approach with these classes. Attendance is up by 50 percent over last year, and we see more cooks and stewards moving up the ladder as a result." To put a number on it, more than two hundred cooks have taken advantage and are enrolled or have graduated from the program since its inception in 2007. Additionally, some Potawatomi employees working outside the food and beverage department have approached Chef Peter because they're interested in taking classes through the Culinary Academy. It's a high compliment when an auxiliary department like F&B self-attracts new talent and enthusiasm.

So, congratulations to the Potawatomi Casino Hotel, Chef Peter Gebauer, and all the team members who have created and completed this promising program. We at *Hotel F&B* magazine will be watching closely and cheering on your accomplishments for what we hope is many years to come.

Jeanne Bischoff
President and Publisher, *Hotel F&B* magazine
Santa Fe, New Mexico
January 2013

hepher EXPRESS

pressmilwaukee.co

NOV. 24, 2010 | FREE

POTAWATOMI'S CULINARY ACADEMY

Introduction

As I am writing these lines, it reminds me of the days going through the interview process here at the casino. A comprehensive and forward-thinking training program with a critical evaluation process attached was one of three major objectives laid out for the new executive chef here, so it was right along "my alley," so speak. By the time you read these words, the Culinary Academy will be in its seventh year and have thirty-one well-established classes in four categories: stewarding; Level One, culinary basics; Level Two, advanced cookery; and Level Three, with specialized classes such as cook chill operation and sous vide cooking.

Designed to be relevant to the business, to support future departmental growth, and to improve career prospects and retention through a dynamic and innovative learning environment, the program has come a long way since March 2007, when we began with six basic classes, including safe knife handling and vegetable cuts, deep fat and pan frying, broiling, grilling, and sautéing.

Then we added more classes especially designed for our team members with the following topics:
Preparations prior to cooking, braising, poaching and steaming, boiling and blanching, stock preparation, and finally roasting.

This curriculum with its twelve classes would run during the first year with one topic per week, times alternating between morning and afternoon sessions to accommodate set working schedules while providing flexibility and the opportunity to participate in this self-paced, forward-thinking program providing a dynamic learning experience and preparing our cooks at the various levels to master the upcoming skills and knowledge tests for cooks at levels one, two, and three.
In 2008 two additional classes, certification at lead and supervisory level, were added, along with the introduction of web-based knowledge testing, growing the program as forecasted.

In 2009 one of our department initiatives was to "go green." I felt that as chefs and professionals, we have an obligation to not only educate our employees, but our guests as well, tackling the issues at stake, getting involved, and being part of the solution. Therefore, as the first of the "advanced curriculum" we developed the Sustainable Foods class, taking a position on our nation's food supply, which is now controlled by a handful of corporations that often put profit ahead of consumer health, the livelihood of the American farmer, the safety of workers, and our own environment.

Later we added advanced cost control, egg cookery, sushi fabrication, and wok cookery, and, in early 2012, cheese making. As for the future, I do have a number of ideas, but it also will depend on how the company will grow and the owners redefine their business goals for this great property.
We will be here to support the vision and mission. As I said once to the vice president of sales in a previous establishment: "You need to bring the guests here, and you have my guarantee that we (food and beverage) will not only meet their expectations, we will also turn them into loyal guests when they leave."

Mission 2006
An empowered culinary team achieving exceptional customer loyalty and financial results by providing flawless service and being best of class.

History

Years ago when opening Star Cruises in Singapore, our strong and effective training programs in food and beverage were the cornerstone for the company's success in achieving brand recognition quickly. In the Asian market we soon grew a reputation of training and developing skilled and knowledgeable cooks and service professionals with a high degree of professionalism, executing total quality service with full engagement. *Genting Star Academy*, as it is called now, is located in Manila, Philippines, and provides innovative competency-based hospitality and development training for professionals as well as newcomers to the hospitality industry.

While at Epcot Center, we would heavily rely on the *Disney Culinary Apprenticeship Program*, accredited by the American Culinary Federation. It was an integral part of food and beverage, with three full-time instructors, an administrative assistant, and many of the chefs in leadership positions functioning as coordinators, adjunct per se.

It was located at Disney's Village Resort, which later became the Villas at Disney Institute.

Walt Disney was, and will always remain, that rare breed: an artistic genius who, with the unflagging and essential support of his brother, Roy, created an effective organizational model and efficient work environment where employees were recognized for their achievements, encouraged to work as a team, and, by striving for excellence, continually broke the confines of the status quo to surpass the expectations of the world. Not only did Walt Disney redefine the world of entertainment, his legacy is found in a worldwide scope of motion pictures, theme parks, stage shows, books, magazines, television, a cruise line, and more.

Since Disney Institute opened in 1986, millions of attendees representing virtually every sector of business from every corner of the globe have had an opportunity to witness and experience these innovative business strategies.

When the DCA ceased operations, culinary classes were integrated into the Disney Institute curriculum for the resort guests; the Institute remains the only professional development company where you will literally step into a "living laboratory" at Disney Theme Parks and Resorts for guided behind-the-scenes field experiences.

Later in Cancun I was able to build onto my training programs during the opening of several resorts and theme parks on the Riviera Maya for Palace Resorts with great success, achieving not only great team member retention but outstanding employee loyalty.

Opryland Culinary Institute

With its opening in 1977, the Opryland Hotel offered a three-year culinary apprenticeship accredited by the American Culinary Federation and administered through the local chapter. In March 1987 the hotel submitted a proposal to administer the apprenticeship in its entirety. The proposal was accepted, and the first class of cooks began training in September of that same year. The program was later named the "Opryland Hotel Culinary Institute." In August 1992, the culinary institute joined hands with Volunteer State Community College in Gallatin, Tennessee, to add an associate of applied science degree to the culinary apprenticeship program. In May 2001, the program was suspended, only to be revived by the newly-named Gaylord Opryland Resort and Convention Center in August 2003 as a partnership with Nashville State Community College.

The program was a year-round, highly structured program consisting of over one thousand hours of theoretical, practical applications and core curriculum intertwined among over six thousand hours of hands-on training in all aspects of food service. Apprentices spend one full day per week in classes and forty hours per week rotating through the various kitchens and restaurants within the Gaylord Opryland Resort and Convention Center complex. The program is divided into three one-year sequences that are classified as "first year," "second year," and "third year," with the move up to the next classification occurring each August when the new class of apprentices arrives.

Upon completion of the culinary apprenticeship program, apprentices graduated as "Certified Culinarian" through the American Culinary Federation, along with receiving the associate of applied science degree in culinary arts and certificates of completion of apprenticeship from the United States Department of Labor and from the American Culinary Federation. The culinary apprenticeship program was administered, governed, and facilitated by Gaylord Opryland Resort and Convention Center, and was registered with the American Culinary Federation and with the United States Department of Labor. The degree component is facilitated through Nashville State Community College, an Equal Opportunity Institution of Higher Learning of the Tennessee State Board of Regents, accredited by the Commission on Colleges of the Southern Association of Colleges and Schools.

The basic purpose of the Gaylord Opryland Culinary Institute was to provide quality education and training for cooks in an attempt to offset an industry wide need for skilled professionals in food service and hospitality, and to instill in each student a sense of the tradition and pride that were longstanding trademarks of Gaylord Opryland. By emphasizing fundamental skills and knowledge with a gradual progression toward the advanced, we created a solid base on which students may expand. Each apprentice was introduced to the history and evolution of the culinary arts so that he or she could appreciate the importance of his or her contribution to our culture. Apprentices are also encouraged in the development of a professional work ethic, which will reflect the quality and style expected of a graduate of the Gaylord Opryland Culinary Institute.

The Gaylord Opryland Resort and Convention Center opened in 1977 with six hundred guest rooms, recently expanding to its current level of 2,881 guest rooms. The hotel boasts of over six hundred thousand square feet of public meeting space, nine acres of gardens under glass, and over three thousand employees. Since its opening, Gaylord Opryland has repeatedly been awarded the Mobile Four Star Award, the AAA Four Diamond Award, and *Meetings & Conventions* magazine's Gold Key Award for operational excellence and outstanding service to guests.

The Culinary Department is staffed with over three hundred employees, including over thirty sous chefs under the leadership of the executive chef, and is part of the Food and Beverage Division, capable of serving over thirty thousand banquet guests in a single day, in addition to preparing food for its eighteen restaurants and food and beverage establishments, five full-service lounges, and twenty retail outlets.

The Admissions Committee was made up of the culinary apprenticeship coordinator, the executive chef, a representative from Nashville State Community College, and a representative from the hotel's training department. Applications were accepted through March of each year, with interviews occurring in April and selections made by May for each class that begins mid-August. Prospective students seeking admission to the Culinary Institute had to meet a number of requirements.

The Culinary Academy

In hands-on training, apprentices should start at square one and learn each skill before moving to another area of the kitchen. All kitchen team members are responsible for ensuring the apprentice learns well; this is accomplished by continual repetitive practice combined with effective coaching. Because of the size of our kitchens, an apprentice will not work in each area of the kitchen to learn the different skills he or she needs to progress. A strong educational component will allow the apprentice to attain those skills.

The Culinary Academy program has grown exponentially in the last year and is about to go into the next phase with an expanded series of classes designed to educate and prepare students for new opportunities as we open new venues and grow in size. With the start of the summer classes, we will also implement a seamless process for all levels of certification. Yes, I assure you of my continued commitment with our certification program, but we need to take it to a higher level so we can plant the seeds for future success.

One of the most vital parts of the culinary education process is chefs that are dedicated to the educational growth of all team members. From the start of their training, we must ensure that there is a strong support system in the kitchens to enable these young people to rely on their chefs for their educational needs.

So, congratulations to all our team members who have already begun to benefit from these classes. The chef who trained me once said that the value of being an apprentice is threefold: it is learning, developing relationships, and, most of all, learning how to communicate and work within a community of chefs and cooks.

Let's work together to continually strengthen the Culinary Academy program so that our team members become better cooks and are prepared for the future, not only here at Potawatomi Casino Hotel but in our profession as well.
June 2007

Philosophy

The main objective of the Culinary Academy is to provide a basic training and educational program for its students. This is achieved by offering participants the opportunity to:

- Develop a personal code of ethics and philosophy to build on the ideals for the student's continuing career.
- Develop a personal sense of pride and professionalism necessary for success in the hospitality industry.
- Develop basic culinary skills so that human and physical resources can be utilized efficiently.
- Understand the principles of food identification and preparation.
- Understand the requirements for proper sanitation in the food service industry.
- Gain a proficient understanding in the use and maintenance of food service equipment.
- Become acquainted with the organization of professional kitchens and bakeshops, and effectively practice basic and advanced skills in food preparation within those kitchens.
- Develop a professional work ethic through a commitment to the Culinary Academy.
- Prepare to demonstrate successfully skills and knowledge to pass the various level certifications set to progress a culinary career internally and externally.
- Gain a general understanding of the culinary field which will serve as a basis for further degree achievements and as a basis for lifelong learning experiences.

It is expected that all culinary apprentices will show courtesy and respect for each other and for all supervisors, instructors, fellow classmates, and team members.

DID YOU KNOW?

When the *Betty Crocker Cook Book* was published by the fictional Betty Crocker in 1950, its sales actually rivaled those of the Bible. Within two years of its publication, the cookbook was in its seventh printing and had sold more than two million copies. The success of the cookbook was due to the beautiful pictures, easy and inexpensive recipes, and practical cooking tips. Now in its eleventh edition and with sixty-five million copies sold (!) one can say that this book shaped the way generations of people cooked.

"If people only knew how hard I work to gain my mastery, It wouldn't seem so wonderful at all."

—*Michelangelo, Italian sculptor*

1

KNIVES

No tools are more identified with chefs than their knives. They must be cared for closely by their owners. They need to be sharpened, cleaned, and handled with respect. Many chefs consider their knives as personal treasures. Today there are so many types and brands of knives that shopping for the best knives may be a trying experience. Following are the steps to help you choose the proper knives for you.

1. First determine your needs; what tasks do you want to accomplish? Do you work with many types of food items or mostly vegetables? Some chefs can perform many functions with just a few versatile knives, an advantage to those on a limited budget.
2. Is the composition of your knives important to you? The materials and method of manufacturing can affect the handling, flexibility, and durability of your knives. The higher the frequency of the ring when you drop a knife, the stronger the steel is. The knife that is stronger will hold its edge longer.
3. What is the value to you of a set of knives? Are you a professional chef or a serious amateur cook? Do you need just a few good knives or a collection that will last a lifetime? Prices vary enormously, and price does not necessarily guarantee quality.
4. The most important point—how do the knives feel to you? Craftsmanship, weight, balance, even the look will all play a role in how you bond with your knives.

Some knives are designed for specific tasks such as slicing or fine-detailed work. The most versatile knife is the chef's or French knife. It is generally eight to fourteen inches long and is used for chopping, slicing, and mincing. A paring knife, which is generally two to four inches long, is used for trimming vegetables and fruits. A boning knife, about six inches long, is thin and ridged, and can work into joints and separate meat from bone. A filet knife for fish is similar in size but more flexible. A slicer is about ten inches long and is used for carving cooked meat. An all-purpose utility knife is about five to seven inches long and is used for light cutting chores. A look at the general design of a chef's knife will help us when looking at other types of knives. The blade is made up of the tip for fine cuts, the middle for chopping and slicing, and the heel to cut through bones and joints. The cutting edge is the business end of the blade. It is formed by wearing the metal away on a grinding machine.

"Flat ground" means that the blade is the same thickness throughout, with a beveled or angled edge ground on. A good edge is a delicate balance between hardness and brittleness.

Hollow ground knives have a concave shape, which may have a sharp edge but will be vulnerable to chipping. A tapered or rounded edge and an edge in which the bevels form an arch shape have the support of the blade metal behind them, offering strength and durability.

The bolster or collar of some knives serves as a barrier between the hand and the blade. The handle is made of wood, a synthetic material like plastic, or some combination of the two. Whether the handle is molded on or secured by rivets, it is important for a knife to have a good grip, especially when the knife is wet. Be sure there are no crevices between the handle and the blade where disease microorganisms might grow.

The tang is the metal part of the knife that extends into the handle. With some exceptions, full-tanged knives are considered sturdier than shorter or welded-together models.

The traditional method of forming a knife from one piece is called the "hot dropped forged" method. Steel is heated to two thousand degrees Fahrenheit and pounded into a mold. After various temperatures and treatments are applied, the steel is set at the proper strength. Because there is a high level of human craftsmanship in the forging technique, these knives tend to be more expensive than those whose shapes are stamped out of a sheet of steel. A stamped knife is generally one thickness of steel.

Carbon steel was the main material in the manufacturing of knives for three thousand years. It sharpens easily but also is prone to staining and rusting. Acidic foods especially bring on these effects. Stainless steel is difficult to sharpen but very durable. It started being used in the early 1900s and has dominated the market for the last forty years.

Manufacturers have now combined the benefits of carbon steel and stainless steel. A well-engineered, high carbon stainless steel knife will take and keep an edge, last long, and resist stain. These new knives have superior performance.

Sharpening

Ongoing care and tuning is what enables knives to carry on their performance. Maintaining sharpness is one of the most important elements for the safe and effective use of knives. A dull edge is dangerous and inefficient. A sharp knife takes less force, so the possibility of slipping is reduced. You will be more productive with a sharp knife because your cuts will be cleaner and quicker. Cutting itself eventually dulls a knife by bending the edge to either side as the blade comes in contact with the food. A lot of cutting or chopping of hard foods, such as root vegetables, will quickly dull the knife. When you notice the deterioration in cutting ability or any worn areas on the blade, you need to sharpen the knife. There are many methods by which to revive the edge of the knife.

Whatever material is used to sharpen the knife must be harder than the blade you are sharpening.

Sharpening stones and honing steels are familiar to most knife owners. Stones, also known as wet stones or bench stones, actually wear away pieces of metal on either side of the edge. Stones are made of natural or manmade substances of varying degrees of hardness. Sharpening removes metal. Sharpen enough to get a good edge, but try to preserve the life of your knife. Honing with steel refines the edge by removing the tiny wire burrs that are formed by the stone abrading the metal. Always steel the knife after sharpening it on a stone. Steels are often used by chefs before they work or before and after each task simply to maintain an edge, not to sharpen. Don't forget to sharpen the bolster so the entire blade can be used.

- -

Sharpening Techniques

1. Some chefs choose to use either water or oil on their stone when sharpening their knife blade. Just spread your choice on the blade.
2. Hold the stone at a vertical angle.
3. Begin at one end of the stone, and move the blade with even pressure forward in one direction. It is recommended that this is done about five times.
4. Then reverse the knife, beginning with the heel, and bring the knife back toward yourself at the same twenty-degree angle with the same amount of pressure.
5. Because the bolster gets in the way during sharpening, it usually leads to the knife not being evenly sharpened. This is why it is a good idea from time to time to have your blade professionally ground.

- -

The choice of many chefs is the multi-oil stone. The advantage to this stone is that it has three replaceable stones in a triangular pattern which offers different levels of coarseness (fine all the way up to rough). Mineral oil should be used with this stone. The sharpening technique with this stone is the same as with other stones; maintain an angle of twenty degrees and use the full length of the stone.

Some chefs prefer the diamond sharpener because they feel it gives them a keener edge. In this sharpening technique, there is no water or oil used. The knife is moved along in a circular motion from the tip all the way to the heel with an even, light pressure. The knife is flipped over, and this process is repeated. Be sure to clean oil and filings off of your knife.

When steeling your knife, always begin with the heel, working with the twenty-degree angle, all the way to the tip. Do not move your arm all over; just use your wrists in the process—hold the steel at arm's length. Always keep your eye on the tip of the steel. Eventually with practice you will speed up.

The steel can also be held in a vertical fashion to sharpen from the heel to the tip in a downward stroke. The blade should be alternated with each stroke, maintaining a twenty-degree angle. Some people feel more comfortable with this due to the possible safety enhancements.

It is important after steeling your knife that it is wiped clean with either soap and water or vinegar, being careful always not to cut yourself.

Some chefs prefer to sharpen in an outward stroke. Just remember, positioning from sharpening to sharpening is very important. Many manufacturers will recommend certain angles to use for their product. A protector can teach you the twenty-degree angle to use. Some sharpeners already have preset angles, taking out any guess work.

KNIVES & USES

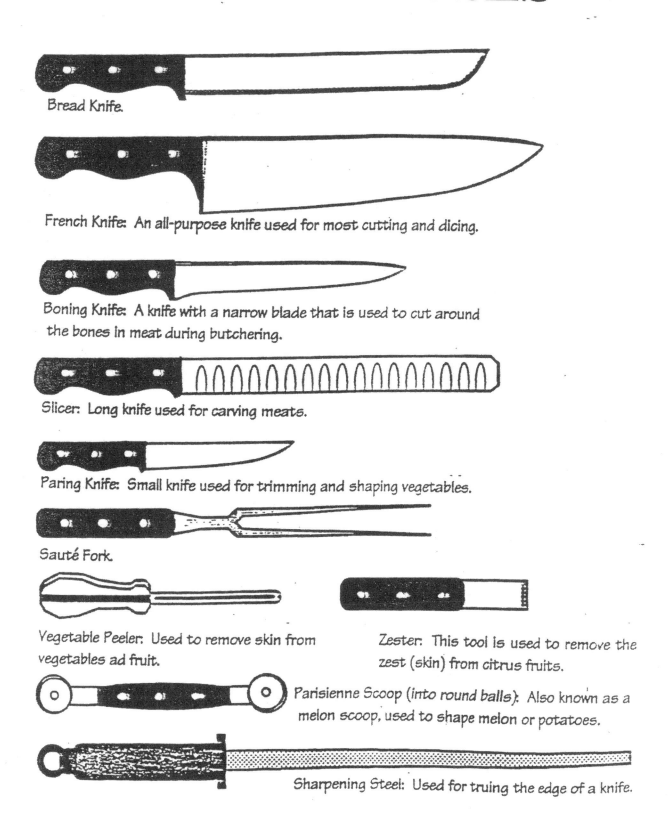

Bread Knife.

French Knife: An all-purpose knife used for most cutting and dicing.

Boning Knife: A knife with a narrow blade that is used to cut around the bones in meat during butchering.

Slicer: Long knife used for carving meats.

Paring Knife: Small knife used for trimming and shaping vegetables.

Sauté Fork.

Vegetable Peeler: Used to remove skin from vegetables ad fruit.

Zester: This tool is used to remove the zest (skin) from citrus fruits.

Parisienne Scoop (into round balls): Also known as a melon scoop, used to shape melon or potatoes.

Sharpening Steel: Used for truing the edge of a knife.

Safety and Etiquette

1. Maintaining sharpness of your knives will prevent too much force from being used, which can cause the knife to slip.
2. Do not sharpen on any surface that was not intended for that purpose.
3. Use your knife on a secure cutting board.
4. Do not expose your knife edge to an inappropriate surface.
5. Hone your knife away from food, and wipe off filings.
6. Do not try to catch a falling knife.
7. Use the correct knife for the job.
8. Stay focused—pay attention to the job at hand.
9. Keep your fingers in a safe position as you cut.
10. Don't reach for a knife anywhere you cannot see it.
11. Pass a knife by its handle or place it down safely first.
12. Don't use your knife on anything but food.
13. Walk with your knife pointed down.
14. Don't move abruptly when you're holding a knife.
15. Above all, use common sense.

Proper Sanitation

As important as safety is proper sanitation. Unclean knives and cutting surfaces are invitations to illness. It is well worth purchasing knives whose handles are seamlessly attached to the metal. After use or between significant tasks, be sure to clean knives thoroughly.

When using a three-compartment sink, follow this recommended procedure.

1. Fill the first sink with detergent and hot water (120°F). Wash your knives well.
2. In the next sink, rinse off the detergent in hot water (130°F).
3. In the third sink, sanitize the knife by submerging it in hot water (170°F) for at least thirty seconds.
4. Then, air dry the knife or wipe it off with a clean towel to resume work.

Do not soak knives too long, as the handles may crack; for the same reason it is advisable to avoid the heat of an electric dishwasher.

Food becomes hazardous to health from spoilage and cross-contamination. Cross-contamination is when undesirable elements are transferred from one food to another. Bacteria, which thrive in protein, warmth, and moisture, are often the illness-causing culprits.

1. Do not use your knife and cutting board, for instance, on a protein food such as poultry and then change directly to another type, such as a vegetable.
2. Both knives and cutting boards should be cleaned in between such different tasks.
3. Be as thorough with plastic boards as you are with wood—microorganisms will thrive where you left them.

Storage and Transport

Your hardworking knives deserve a fitting storage place. Be aware of safety and sanitation when you choose a way to store and transport your knives. Racks, drawers, and blocks with individual slots will protect the knives, but the slots must be kept clean. Magnetized racks must be strong enough for the heaviest knives and positioned in a safe place. For transport, kits and cases are convenient, but make sure that no tip of blade can break through. The briefcase style is heavier but sturdier.

> **NOTE:**
> *Knives are the tools of the trade. They should be respected and maintained at all times. Without a sharp knife, it is very difficult to do a professional job. Knives demand attention, but if you provide it, they will provide for a lifetime.*

Standard Vegetable Cuts

Definition

The purpose of cutting vegetables is to make them uniform in shape and size in order for them to cook evenly with an attractive appearance. Use of quality product and timing—preparation as close to the cooking time as possible—are important, as is the selection of the right tools for the best results.

Julienne	⅛ x ⅛ x 1–2 inches
Batonet	¼ x ¼ x 2 inches
Brunoise	⅛ x ⅛ x ⅛ inch
Small dice	¼ x ¼ x ¼ inch
Medium dice	½ x ½ x ½ inch
Large dice	¾ x ¾ x ¾ inch
Paysanne	½ x ½ x ⅛ inch
Lozenge/diamond	½ x ½ x ⅛ inch
Tourné	Approximately 2 inches with 7 faces
Oblique or roll cut	Primarily used with cylindrical vegetables—cut diagonally (90 degrees), then roll the item ¼ turn and cut diagonal again; repeat

PBC CULINARY ACADEMY

LEVEL 2: ADVANCED

1st Semester Schedule – 2013

SUSTAINABLE VISION........................... *CLASS HELD IN F&B CONFERENCE ROOM*	JANUARY 30	9 AM
MISSION: COST CONTROL........................ *CLASS HELD IN F&B CONFERENCE ROOM*	FEBRUARY 20	9 AM
CHEESE MAKING................................. *CLASS HELD IN DREAM DANCE STEAK KITCHEN*	MARCH 20	9 AM
SUSHI 101...................................... *CLASS LOCATION TBD*	APRIL 17	9 AM
EGG COOKERY................................... *CLASS LOCATION TBD*	MAY 15	9 AM
WOK COOKERY.................................. *CLASS HELD IN RUYI KITCHEN*	JUNE 19	9 AM
ITALIAN 101.................................... *CLASS HELD IN F&B CONFERENCE ROOM*	JULY 17	9 AM

DID YOU KNOW?

Georges Auguste Escoffier

Proclaimed the "king of chefs, chef of kings," Escoffier was a French-born chef and restaurateur who revolutionized both his profession and the public's palate nearly one hundred years ago. His impact still resonates today. To him goes credit for making dining a la carte popular; inventing cherries jubilee (in honor of Queen Victoria) and Melba toast (for the Australian opera singer Nellie Melba); organizing restaurant kitchens along quasi-military lines; and, so it is said, offering career advice to a young kitchen worker from Vietnam named Ho Chi Minh.

Shortly before his death in 1935 at age eighty-eight, Escoffier was being called a "super chef."

REVIEW QUESTIONS

1. What is considered the most versatile knife?

2. What is the paring knife generally used for?

3. Explain the difference between a filet knife and a boning knife.

4. Explain the use of the following parts of the knife:

   a   Tip

   b   Middle

   c   Heel

5. What is the purpose of the bolster/collar?

6. What is the tang?

7. What makes a dull knife dangerous?

8. When sharpening a knife, which needs to be stronger—the knife or the material being used to sharpen the knife?

9. Should one steel a knife before or after sharpening it on a stone?

10. When steeling a knife, what part of the knife should you begin with?

11. After steeling a knife, what should you always do?

12. When passing a knife, what part should it be passed with?

13. What is cross-contamination?

14. What should you look for when choosing ways to store and transport your knives?

15. When should knives be cleaned?

16. What is *chiffonade*?

17. What types of *mirepoix* do you know?

18. What is *matignon*?

"Everything is relative but there is a standard which must not be deviated from, especially with reference to the basic culinary preparations."

Auguste Escoffier

2

SAUTÉ

Definition

The cooking technique known as *sautéing* is a high-heat cooking method used primarily with portion-sized cuts of tender meat, fish, and poultry. Predominantly a range-top cooking method, sautéed items, especially larger cuts such as chicken breasts or tournedos of beef, may need to be finished in the oven, covered or uncovered. On the stovetop, all sautéed items are cooked in a preheated skillet or sauté pan.

A *sauteuse* has gently curving sides, while a *sautoir* has straight sides.

A small amount of fat, oil, or clarified butter is an essential component of the sauté cooking method. Fat acts as a searing agent and adds significant flavor to the sautéed item. The pan and fat must be quite hot in order to avoid excess absorption of fat and to prevent accumulation of moisture in the pan. A major consideration of sautéing is the problem of moisture accumulation. If moisture is allowed to accumulate in the pan during the sauté process, meat and fish lose juices, start to boil, and become tough.

To prevent accumulation of moisture:
- Make sure the pan and fat are sufficiently hot.
- Ensure that the meat or fish is totally dry.
- Dredge the poultry or fish in flour.
- When the item is placed in the pan, it should be left alone until the heat has recovered.
- Once the heat has recovered, the item should be sautéed quickly.

The three essential components necessary for sautéing are:
1. The main products: portion-sized cuts
2. The searing agent: oils or clarified butter
3. Liquids: deglazing or sauce bases

There are three optional components which may be used when sautéing:
1. Flavoring (herbs, spices, condiments, liqueurs)
2. Finishing (butter, cream, glace)
3. Garnishing

When added to the essential components, optional components help to define the character of the dish.

Proper ***mise en place*** is essential for ***all*** cooking methods.
>Sauté pan and clarified butter
>Chicken breast
>Flour
>Minced shallots
>White wine
>Veal glace

Cream
Chives or tarragon
Salt and pepper

1. Sautéed items should be absolutely dry before being placed in the pan. Sautéed foods should remain moist and tender on the inside while they develop a light crust on the surface.
2. Items should be seasoned prior to sautéing. Fish and poultry should be dredged in enough flour to provide a uniform, thin coating, which aids in creating the proper color and protects the flesh, as well as sealing in the juices of the item.
3. At high heat, almost no moisture escapes from the item into the pan. Be aware that a deep pan or skillet will trap moisture, interfering with browning. A thin pan of lighter gauge steel or aluminum may lend itself to burning. The pan must be large enough to hold all of the food in a single layer. A pan that is too large will have gaps between the items, causing hot spots and burning. A pan that is too small will cause the accumulation of moisture and possible undercooking. As a safety precaution, make sure that the pan is tipped away from you, and the food in the pan is placed toward the cooking surface so that the fat does not splash in your direction.
4. When the food is placed in the pan, the temperature of the fat drops. The item should not be stirred, turned, or lifted until the heat has recovered to its original temperature. When the heat has recovered, and the item has cooked sufficiently, turn the item toward the back of the pan to avoid splatter burns.
5. Sautéing is an *a la minute* cooking method. Each dish is made to order. Sautéed items are turned only once. For white meat and fish, turn the item when it exhibits a golden brown color known as *"dore."* Red meat should have a medium to dark brown color. After browning the first side, the item may be finished in the oven at medium high heat, depending on the dish.
6. Using your finger, test for resilience as this is the key to the doneness of the piece of meat. Proper color is the single most important factor in determining doneness. When the item is done, remove it from the pan along with any excess fat. Sautéed items lose heat quickly, so it is important to keep the item warm while you begin the deglazing process.
7. Deglazing is an essential part of sautéing red and white meats. Deglazing often uses wine and stock as deglazing liquids, and these should be compatible with the sautéed item. For example, if the sautéed item is chicken, white wine would be an appropriate deglazing liquid. Since fish creates no useable fond, sautéed fish dishes are usually accompanied by a butter-based sauce. White and red meats are served with a sauce made by deglazing the fonds. Fonds are the caramelized liquids formed by the drippings in the pan.
8. After the item is cooked and the excess fat is poured off, return the pan to medium heat, being careful not to burn the fond. Add garniture, such as shallots, and sauté lightly. When the shallots turn golden or translucent, add the deglazing liquid.
   Loosen the fond from the pan, and add the other ingredients for the deglazed sauce, then add the veal glace and the cream to the pan and reduce. Then the herbs are added.
9. It is important to taste the sauce to see it is properly seasoned.
10. The sautéed item may be placed on the service plate, or returned to the pan to absorb the heat and flavor of the sauce. Be careful not to boil the sauce—simply blend and reheat.
    Depending on the dish, the sauce may be finished either under or over the item. In either case, use enough sauce to lubricate the sautéed item. A single portion will usually call for no more than a two-ounce ladle. Serve at once.

Review

The cooking technique known as sautéing is a high heat cooking method, used primarily with portion-sized cuts of tender meat, fish, and poultry. Sautéing is a stove-top cooking method, so some sautéed items, especially larger cuts such as chicken breasts and tournedos of beef, may need to be finished in the oven.

The essentials of sautéing are:

    The main products: portion-sized cuts of meat, poultry, and fish
    Searing agents/fats: oils or clarified butter
    Liquids: for deglazing and sauce bases

The optional components of sautéing are:

    Flavoring (herbs, spices, condiments, liqueurs)
    Finishing (butter, cream, glace)
    Garnishing

All white meats, poultry, and fish should be dredged in flour prior to sautéing. This will create a golden brown color and become the fond for deglazing. Since sautéed fish items create no useable fond for deglazing, sauces for fish are usually butter based, such as *meuniere.*

The sequence of sautéing:

1. Gather the *mise en place*.
2. Heat the pan and the fat.
3. Season the item to be sautéed.
4. All fish, poultry, and white meats must be dredged in flour prior to placing in the pan.
5. When the pan and fat are hot, add the sautéed item.
6. Sauté without touching the item until it appears to be golden brown.
7. Turn the item only once.
8. Continue to cook the item until done; test by touching with your finger and observe the color of the item.
9. Remove the item from the pan and place on a service dish.
10. Deglaze the pan, using the appropriate liquid and finishing ingredients.
11. Pour the sauce on the plate, or place the sautéed item in the pan to absorb the flavor and heat of the sauce, and serve immediately.

Summary for Sautéing

Quickly cooking foods in a small amount of oil with high heat

Suitable foods are: beef, veal, pork, lamb, poultry, seafood, and vegetables

Remember:

Be sure items to be cooked are tender, and *do not*:

- Overcrowd the pan (moisture toughens the protein).
- Add items to a pan that is not at the right temperature (causes moisture buildup).
- Add too much or too little oil.
- Cover the pan (causes steaming and toughens the product).

Equipment Needs

A shallow sauté pan

Tongs

Roasting fork

Spatulas to turn items

Wire rack to drain product

Procedure

1. Bone, trim, portion, and season.
2. Preheat proper amount of oil.
3. Dry item, dredge with flour, and add to hot oil.
4. When browned, turn to other side to brown.
5. Cook to required internal temperature.
6. Item may be finished off in the oven.
7. Remove item and keep warm for service.

Laughing Bird Shrimps over Stone Ground Grits with Wisconsin Cheddar and Red Eye Gravy
Yield: 4 servings
My preferred grits comes from Oak view Farm, a family-owned gristmill in Wetumpka, Alabama. There is absolutely no comparison in nutrients, flavor, and quality with freshly ground corn and wheat vs. commercial degerminated varieties. Always buy local and from a producer you know.

Ingredients:
2 cups/16 ounces vegetable stock
Kosher salt and pepper to taste
Juice from half a lemon
½ cup/4 ounces stone ground organic grits
½ cup/4 ounces aged cheddar cheese, shredded
1 pound shrimp, peeled and deveined, tail on
¼ cup/2 ounces canola oil
1 garlic glove, peeled and crushed
1 plum tomato, seeded, small diced
¼ cup/2 ounces brewed coffee
½ stick/2 ounces unsalted butter
1 bunch chives, sliced
1 teaspoon flaxseeds, crushed

Prepare the grits:
In a shallow pot bring 2 cups of stock/water to a boil. Add salt to taste.
Stir in the grits, cover, and let simmer for 20 minutes, stirring occasionally.
Add the grated cheddar; turn off the heat and cover.
After 10 minutes check the taste and consistency.

Prepare the shrimp:
1. Season the shrimp with lemon juice, salt, and pepper.
2. Heat a pan and add the oil.
3. Add the garlic and tomato to roast briefly on high heat.
4. Add the shrimp and stir fry briefly.
5. Deglaze with the coffee and cook until the shrimp are done.
6. Finish with fresh butter, chives, and flaxseeds to build the sauce.

NOTE:
Plate as desired and garnish with sliced chives and flaxseeds.

DID YOU KNOW?

Laughing Bird Key off the coast of Belize was named after the laughing gull known to nest there. Just a few miles inland is located what experts have deemed "the future of aquaculture," a result of years of thoughtful environmental design. This remarkable, low-impact operation produces an incredibly flavorful, succulent shrimp favored by environmentalists and seafood lovers alike.

REVIEW QUESTIONS

1. What types of food items are best suited for sautéing?

2. What are the three essential components of sautéing?

3. What are the three optional components of sautéing?

4. What type of pan is best used for sautéing? What size?

5. What are the four techniques to prevent the accumulation of moisture while sautéing?

6. What will happen to the sautéed item if moisture accumulates?

7. What is the importance of dredging sautéed items in flour prior to sautéing?

8. Why must sautéed items be completely dry before sautéing?

9. Why must you use high heat when sautéing?

10. When the item has been placed in the hot pan, how often do you turn it? Explain your answer.

11. How do you test for doneness of a sautéed item?

12. Describe the process to deglaze a pan.

13. What type of sauce is made for sautéed fish?

14. Why do the sauces for sautéed fish differ from the sauces for sautéed meat and poultry?

15. What types of liquids are used for deglazing?

16. List three examples of finishing ingredients.

17. Can sautéed items be prepared in advance and reheated prior to service?

"**When you have confidence, you can have a lot of fun. And when you have fun, you can do amazing things.**"

Joe Namath

3

FRY

Definition
Deep fat frying and pan frying are essentially dry heat cooking methods. Fat in its liquid state is used as the cooking medium. The hot fat quickly sears the surface, sealing in the natural juices and cooking the interior of the item. The characteristics of fried foods are a crisp, brown exterior with a tender, moist interior.

Mise en place for deep fat frying:
Main item
Cooking medium
Standard breading: egg wash (eggs and milk), flour, and bread crumbs or batter
Seasoning: salt and pepper, lemon juice, soy sauce

Common deep fat fry items include chicken, fish, onions, shrimps, and soft vegetables such as squash, eggplant, and zucchini.

Deep Fat Frying with Batter
1. Shrimp is used as the main item to demonstrate the method for deep fat frying with batter.
2. Shrimp are deveined, patted dry, and seasoned.
3. The shrimp are then coated with flour, which helps the batter adhere to the item.
4. Once dipped into the prepared batter, the shrimp will be added to the hot fat immediately.
5. To ensure that the fat is hot enough, hold the tip of the shrimp in the fat. If correct, release the shrimp carefully.
6. Finished items are then removed by a skimmer, held for a moment to allow draining of the fat, and then placed on absorbent toweling. Any small particles left in the hot fat must be removed, as these will burn and cause premature deterioration of the fat. This can be costly and result in poor-tasting product.

> **NOTE:**
> *Always proceed with caution to avoid the spattering of hot fat. Deep fat frying requires enough fat to submerge the item. Once the item is sealed, the internal moisture is heated and actually steams the interior of the item.*
> *While cooking, the temperature of the fat must be maintained at 350°F. The item is allowed to swim and must be gently turned once with tongs or a spider to ensure even browning.*
> *When not in use, lower the temperature to 200°F.*

With chicken or fish:

Egg wash is used after the flouring stage to allow the bread crumbs to stick to the item. Blend the eggs and liquid together, and beat to achieve the proper consistency. If the egg wash is too thin, it will not create the proper base to allow the breading to adhere, resulting in a coating that will not seal properly.

Keep one hand dry during the breading process. Avoid layering, sticking, or touching items together.

1. The item—a boneless chicken breast—should be patted dry of any excess moisture.
2. The chicken is first seasoned with salt and pepper, followed by a light coating of flour.
3. Place in the egg wash next, and then bread crumbs.
   Placing the coating ingredients in a line will make the process an easy and continuous motion. Any coating should be evenly applied, and special care should be taken not to damage this layer before or during the early stages of the frying process.
4. When the fryer has reached the appropriate temperature, the item may be placed in the fat. If too many items are added at one time, the temperature of the fat will drop too quickly. Foods that have been breaded can be placed in a wire basket away from the fryer so that any loose particles do not fall into the fryer.
5. The basket is then lowered into the fat and lifted out when the food is properly done. If the fat is too cool and the item fried too slowly, it will not be properly sealed, resulting in a soggy and greasy product. If the fat is too hot, the item will prematurely brown, and the food may still be raw inside. Since internal moisture and pressure can render a soggy crust in a very short time, the food should be served immediately to retain the qualities and characteristics of fried foods—crisp outside, tender and juicy inside.

The frying fat must be maintained and monitored during all stages of the cooking process.
Heating beyond the smoking temperature can cause breakdown of the fat by oxidation, or by burned particles.
If the fat smokes at or below 300°F, it must be discarded.
It the fat smells strong, then it is probably too old to use.

Deep fat frying vegetables:

Vegetables should be washed and thoroughly dried. They should be cut appropriately so that when the crust is browned, the vegetable will be properly cooked. A similar breading procedure is used for the coating. The fat must reach its correct temperature before frying and regain its temperature between batches. Many factors determine what the temperature should be, such as the size and shape of the item and the recovery time of the fryer.
If salting is required, it must not be done over the fryer. That will assist in rapid breakdown. Properly deep fat fried foods should have a crisp exterior, a golden color, and no traces of excess greasiness or heaviness.

> **NOTE:**
> *The fat in the deep fat fryer in the kitchen is a big investment. It is very costly to replace the fat in the fryer, depending on the size of the fryer. If the fat isn't used or taken care of properly, its usable life is greatly shortened. Exposure to the wrong types of items, such as bacon that has free fatty acids, causes the rapid breakdown of fat. Items with too high a moisture content also have a negative impact on the fryer and the fat. The maintenance of a deep fat fryer is essential. Cooks often do not realize how expensive the oil is and do not take care of the fat. If the fat is strained after every shift and refilled, the usable life of the fat can be well extended.*
>
> *The poor taste of some deep fat fried items can be the result of fat that has gone past its usable life. The fat at this point requires the temperature to be higher to prevent the absorption of fat into the crust. This creates fat that can burn and create soggy products.*

Remember:

Although the fat used for the frying will influence the flavor of the item being fried, deep fat fried foods should taste like the item prepared, not like the fat used to fry the food, or like other foods that have been previously fried in the same fat. The flavor of the fat should be neutral.

Common Oil Properties

	Percentage of Specific Types of Fat			
Oils	**Saturated**	**Monounsaturated**	**Polyunsaturated**	**Trans**
Canola	7	58	29	0
Safflower	9	12	74	0
Sunflower	10	20	66	0
Corn	13	24	60	0
Olive	13	72	8	0
Soybean	16	44	37	0
Peanut	17	49	32	0
Rice Bran**	20	47	33	0
Cottonseed***	25	17	58	0
Palm	50	37	10	0
Coconut	87	6	2	0
Cooking Fats				
Shortening	22	29	29	18
Lard	39	44	11	1
Butter	60	26	5	5
Margarine/Spreads				
Imperial 70% Soybean Stick	18	2	29	23
Fleischmann 67% Spread, Corn and Soybean Tub	16	27	44	11
Shedd's Country Crock 48% Spread, Soybean Tub	17	24	49	8
Promise 60% Tub, Sunflower, Soybean, and Canola	18	22	54	5

*Values expressed as percent of total fat.
From Harvard School of Public Health and USDA publications.

DID YOU KNOW?

Crisco

This brand of shortening was introduced in June 1911 by Procter & Gamble. It was the first shortening to be made entirely of vegetable oil. The term *Crisco* is comes from "crystallized cottonseed oil" and is commonly used as a synonym for all shortening. As of 2012, Crisco consists of a blend of soybean oil and hydrogenated palm oil.

Method for Pan Frying:

Chicken Breast:

1. The standard breading procedure is used: flour, egg wash, and bread crumbs. Aside from the standard breading, there are a number of options depending on the desired taste of the final product. Cornmeal is one example. Cornmeal can be used in combination with other products, such as chopped nuts or coconut. Specialty flours, such as rye or wheat flours, may be substituted.

The pan used in this method of frying must be able to withstand exposure to prolonged heat, transfer heat evenly, and also be large enough to ensure the proper ratio of fat to the cooking item.

1. Touch the corner of the chicken to the fat to ensure that the fat has reached the proper temperature. Be sure that the cooking medium has reached the correct temperature before introducing any additional items into the pan. Use caution when cooking with hot fats.
2. When initial browning of the outer surface has taken place, lower the temperature. The item can then be turned to ensure even cooking. Keeping the items in motion will maintain a layer of fat between the pan and the item. This will prevent sticking. A sautoir, with its straight sides, or a cast iron skillet is recommended for safe handling of hot fats.

An important element influencing the final flavor of fried foods is the type of fat used. It should be neutral in flavor so that it does not interfere with the flavor of the food. The chicken is then removed, drained briefly on absorbent toweling, and served immediately.

Deep Fat Frying and Pan Frying Review

Deep Fat Frying with Batter:

1. Clean and cut the item to appropriate size.
2. Apply seasonings.
3. Apply a light coating of flour.
4. Dip item in batter, then into the hot fat immediately. Test temperature by touching corner of the item into the fat.
5. Turn items being fried halfway through cooking.
6. Remove items with skimmer, hold, and let drain on toweling.
7. Skim particles of batter from fat.
8. Serve immediately.

Deep Fat Frying with Breading:

1. Clean and cut item to appropriate size. Pat dry.
2. Apply seasonings.
3. Coat item with flour, egg wash, and breading.
4. Use a wire basket to lower items into hot fat (350°F).
5. Turn items during frying.
6. When golden brown, remove items, drain on toweling. Salt the item away from the fryer.
7. Serve immediately.

Pan Frying with Breading:

1. Clean and cut item to appropriate size. Pat dry.
2. Apply seasonings.
3. Coat item with flour, egg wash, and breading.
4. Place in *sautoir* or skillet with thin layer of fat.
5. Check temperature. Look for haze or touch corner of item to hot fat. Avoid overcrowding.
6. Turn items halfway through cooking.
7. When golden brown, serve immediately

DID YOU KNOW?

Pan frying and deep frying is not suitable for healthy cooking. Due to the fat absorption into the crust, deep fat frying is not recommended by nutritional guidelines. Unfortunately today, deep fat frying is the most common technique for the average meal because it does not require a great deal of cooking skill and knowledge. If the fat is the right temperature, and the item is prepared correctly and consistently, it is easy to use this technique. After preparation, the item need only be placed in the fat for the required amount of time, and it will be cooked. It is a reliable cooking method in fast-food operations and one of the most prevalent in the United States.

Beer Batter
Yield: **4 to 6 servings**

Ingredients:
10 ounces all-purpose flour
½ teaspoon baking powder
1 teaspoon salt
1 egg
10 ounces beer

Preparation:
1. Whisk together dry ingredients.
2. Separate egg. Add egg yolk and beer at once and whisk until smooth.
3. Whip egg white to a soft peak and fold into batter.
4. Use at once.

Asian Dipping Sauce
Yield: **20 servings of 2 ounces**

Ingredients:
16 ounces light soy sauce
12 ounces red miso
8 ounces Mirin
1 ounce sesame seeds
2 ounces sesame paste
2 ounces brown sugar
1 tablespoon Sri Racha chili sauce

Preparation:
1. Mix all ingredients in a stainless steel bowl.
2. Refrigerate until service.

DID YOU KNOW?

The color of a chili pepper actually has nothing to do with its heat level. Rather, the color typically signifies the maturity of the fruit. Chiles generally change from green in color during growth to a variety of colors at maturity—yellow, brown, orange, and typically red. For example, a jalapeño is green during growth and typically harvested and sold green in color, but, left on the plant to mature, it turns to red. Another example—a cayenne pepper is green during its growth, but turns red when it reaches maturity.

A chipotle chili is a smoke-dried jalapeño pepper.

Indian Fry Bread
Yield: 16 breads

Many Native Americans eat fry bread with almost every meal. It is found at all public Indian events, including dances, pow wows, etc. You can usually buy the fry bread at these events plain with powdered sugar on it or made into an Indian taco.

Ingredients:
4 cups all-purpose flour
2 tablespoons baking powder
1 teaspoon salt
2 cups water
Vegetable shortening or oil for frying

Preparation:
1. Mix the flour, baking powder, and salt in a large bowl.
2. Gradually stir in the water until the dough becomes soft and pliable without sticking to the bowl.
3. Knead the dough on a lightly floured surface or in the bowl for 5 minutes, folding the outer edges of the dough toward the center.
4. Return the dough to the bowl, cover with a clean towel, and let rest 30 minutes to allow the dough to rise.
5. Shape the dough into egg-size balls and roll out on a lightly floured board to a thickness of ½ inch (or thinner, for crispier bread). It is traditional to use your hands, but a rolling pin may be used.
6. Place a piece of dough between your hands and pat it from hand to hand as you would a tortilla or pizza dough, until it has stretched to 8 to12 inches in diameter. Repeat with the rest of the dough.
7. With your finger, poke a small air hole in the center of each piece, to prevent bursting during frying.
8. Pour approximately 1½ inches of oil into a large frying pan or saucepan and heat over medium heat until the oil is hot (350°F) but not smoking.
9. Carefully place a piece of the dough in the hot oil, slipping it in gently to avoid splattering. Cook until the dough turns golden brown and puffs. Turn over and cook until both sides are golden brown.
10. Remove and drain on paper towels until the excess oil is absorbed. Repeat this process with each piece of dough.
11. Keep warm between two clean towels in the oven on low. Serve immediately.

Suppli al Telefono (Fried Rice Balls Roman Style)
Yield: 18 rice balls

Rice Ingredients:
¼ cup extra-virgin olive oil
½ cup diced onion
1 cup   jasmine rice
1¾ cups chicken stock, unsalted
To taste: kosher salt and freshly ground black pepper
1 ounce fresh basil leaves, cut chiffonade (need 1 cup)
1 egg yolk, beaten
1 cup   Scamorza cheese, grated
½ cup smoked provolone, grated

Rice Preparation:
1. Heat a large ovenproof saucepan over medium heat. Add olive oil and heat.
2. Add onion and sauté until translucent.
3. Add rice and bay leaf and sauté until grains of rice are glistening, 1–2 minutes.
4. Add chicken stock, salt, and pepper. At this point, mixture should be a little over seasoned.
5. Preheat oven to 375ºF.
6. Bring mixture to a boil and cover with an oiled sheet of parchment paper.
7. Transfer to preheated oven and cook 16–18 minutes, until all liquid is absorbed.
8. Take a 2-pronged roasting fork and fluff the rice. Transfer to a shallow baking dish.
9. When cool, mix in basil, egg yolk, and cheeses, and season to taste with salt and pepper.

Suppli Ingredients:
5 ounces Tallegio cheese, rind removed, cut into 18 (½–¾-inch) cubes
1 cup all purpose flour
2 eggs, beaten
1½ cups bread crumbs
Fried basil leaves, for garnish, optional

Preparation:
1. Divide rice mixture into 18 (1½-inch) balls by placing a heaping tablespoon of the mixture in the palm of your hand and firmly squeezing into a ball, then flattening slightly.
2. Place a cube of the Tallegio in the center of each portion of the rice mixture and reform into a ball. At this point balls will measure about 2 inches in diameter.
3. Refrigerate rice balls until firm, about 20 minutes.
4. When rice balls are firm, dredge each ball in flour, then lightly pat to remove excess flour
5. Next, dip rice balls in eggs and remove from pan with a wide fork to drain off excess egg wash.
6. Transfer to dish with bread crumbs and gently roll to coat completely.
7. Set the breaded balls on a parchment-lined cookie sheet.
8. In a large, wide pan that is at least 4 inches deep, heat enough olive oil to cover suppli to 350ºF.
9. Fry 4–5 minutes, turning once, or until golden brown and hot in center.
10. Remove from hot oil and set on paper toweling to drain briefly.
11. Serve hot, garnished with fried basil leaves if desired.

NOTE:

Scamorza is a stretched curd cheese in which the fresh curd matures in its own whey for several hours to allow acidity to develop by the process. Scamorza is made more in the south and can be substituted by mozzarella.

REVIEW QUESTIONS

1. Briefly describe the pan frying and deep fat frying methods.

2. What are the characteristics of food that has been fried properly?

3. What is the standard breading procedure?

4. True or false: The temperature of the fat when frying must be a moderate temperature, approximately 300ºF.

5. Why is the temperature of the fat so important?

6. How should meat items, such as chicken, be prepared for deep fat frying?

7. It is recommended that overcrowding of the pan be avoided when pan frying. Why?

8. What is the procedure for deep fat frying fish?

9. What is important to remember when salting fried foods? Why?

10. Explain the proper maintenance of fat in a deep fat fryer.

11. How can you tell if the fat is too old to be used?

12. When items will be fried, it is recommended that they be trimmed and then patted dry. Why is it important to dry the items?

13. If items touch each other during the breading process, what will happen during the frying process?

14. After removing an item from the sautoir or deep fat fryer, what is done prior to service? Why?

15. What are two clues that the fat in the pan is hot enough for pan frying?

> *"It is pointless to say:*
> *We do our best.*
> *We must succeed*
> *to do what is*
> *necessary."*

Winston Churchill

4

BRAISE

Definition

Braising is a cooking method that combines both dry and moist heat. In this process the meat is first seared to brown and enhance the flavor. It is then slowly simmered in liquid to break down the connective tissues and make it tender. Properly braised cuts should have a rich brown appearance outside and be tender yet firm inside, with plenty of savory juices. Braising can be done on top of a stove or in the oven.

It is the best cooking method for preparing less-tender cuts of meat and poultry, such as the shank, shoulder, and brisket. Braising makes these cuts more tender and flavorful. Braising is also a suitable method for beef, lamb, poultry, game, and offal.

Large pieces of meat as well as individual cuts can be braised successfully, including such items as Swiss steak, stew meats, brisket, and shanks. Sufficient fat outside and marbleization throughout the meat provide the necessary basting medium.

Mise en place for braising:

Beef knuckle	Braising pan
Oil	Fat back or larding needle
Salt and pepper	Aromatics
Mirepoix	Tomato product
Brown stock	Cheesecloth for *sachet d'epices* and straining
Cornstarch	

About braising:

1. First select the pot into which the meat will fit properly. It should not be crowded or too spacious. This will assure proper moisture retention and reduce shrinkage. Any deep pot with a tight-fitting domed lid is suitable.
2. With cuts such as beef knuckle or bottom round that are deficient in fat or marbleization, larding may be necessary to keep the meat from drying out during the braising process. A cut such as beef brisket, sufficient in fat, may not require larding.
3. *Larding* is an option in the braising process.
4. The meat is dried thoroughly to aid in the caramelization and to prevent the splattering that occurs as a result of surface moisture.
5. Next, season the meat; salt and pepper are usually all that is necessary. By rubbing the seasonings in, the meat is penetrated, enhancing the flavor throughout the cut. Dredging is may be used for portion-sized cuts to enhance color.
6. The meat is then placed fat side down into the hot oil. The temperature should be high enough to brown but not burn. Important factors in the searing process are controls in the amount of fat and temperature control. All sides of the meat should be seared evenly and turned with a fork by the fatty part so that no juices are lost. The meat should caramelize to a rich brown. The fond in the bottom of the pot should not be burned. The meat should now be removed from the pot.

7. Now a *mirepoix* of carrots and onions is added to the fat to caramelize. The amount is dependent upon the amount of meat braised. The ratio is one ounce of *mirepoix* to one pound of meat. The celery is added a little later, as it has high water content and hinders caramelization.

8. A tomato product is introduced to add flavor and color. A small amount of stock is added to deglaze the fond. Wine, beer, or other flavorful liquids may be substituted for stock in specific applications, such as removing a gamy taste from a meat like wild venison.

9. Now, a greater amount of liquid is added—the amount is dependent upon the number of portions the cut will yield, about three to five ounces per portion.

10. The meat is returned to the pot and brought to a simmer, a lazy bubble to maintain slow cooking. Boiling the meat will result in shrinkage and drying, and the sauce will appear unclear. The cooking medium should almost engulf the meat, coming to about two inches from the top of it.

11. A *sachet d'epices* of items such as crushed peppercorns, clove, thyme, bay leaf, and parsley stems, is placed into the stock to add flavor.

12. Once the lid is replaced, the meat can be left on top of the stove to simmer or placed in the oven. If placed in the oven, the meat should be checked often to make sure proper simmering is taking place at a proper rate.

13. Occasional turning assures even cooking. Larger cuts can be left to simmer for two to two-and-a-half hours and smaller cuts one-and-a-half to two hours.

14. To check for doneness, a fork is inserted into the meat. If it goes in and comes out easily, the meat is done.

15. The meat is now removed from the sauce. It should be covered and held aside on a warming shelf at a temperature of about 135ºF until service. To prevent it from drying out, a small amount of stock is placed in the holding vessel and then covered.

16. The sauce is strained through cheesecloth to remove the *mirepoix* and bits of seasoning.

17. The sauce must now be allowed to settle so the fat may come to the surface and be removed. This process is called *degrassier*.

18. The sauce is returned to a proper-sized pot and returned to a simmer, additional fat and impurities are skimmed off until the sauce is clear. This process is known as *depouillage*.

19. For thickening, a starch, such as arrowroot or cornstarch, and cold water are combined for a slurry.

20. A slurry will thicken a sauce more quickly than a roux. Taste and adjust seasonings to taste.

21. Now is the time to slice the meat. It should be sliced against the grain and the texture should be tender yet firm, and the juices clear and plentiful. The portion size should range from three to four ounces and no more than two ounces of sauce served over the meat.

Braising Review

Meals that are both flavorful and cost effective can be readily obtained if the basics of braising are adhered to.
-The meat is of a suitable size and cut.
-The pot provides a proper fit for moisture retention
-The meat should be dried, seasoned, and seared thoroughly in a small amount of oil.
-There should be an adequate cooking medium and temperature for simmering.
-The finished braise should be fork tender and the juices clear.

Essentials for braising:

-Flavoring ingredients—*mirepoix* and also other herbs, spices, or fruits
-Thickening agents—roux, modified starches, potatoes, gingersnaps, bread crumbs, blood

Optional components include:

-Finishing ingredients, such as cream, sour cream, *liaison*
-Garnish
-Larding leaner cuts of meat
-Marinating, leading to tenderizing and reducing any game flavors in the meat

Procedure:

1. Dry the product.
2. Season the product.
3. Sear the product, and then remove from the heat.
4. Caramelize *mirepoix* and then add tomato product.
5. Add liquid and aromatics.
6. Return to heat and cover tightly.
7. Simmer slowly until "fork tender."
8. Strain.
9. Degrease sauce—adjust consistency and taste of stock if needed.
10. Hold in small amount of stock, covered.
11. Serve.

It is important to remember the proper braising ratios:
For every pound of protein we use a small amount of the searing medium, 6 to 10 ounces of cooking liquids, and 1 ounce of *mirepoix*.
The ratios of the remaining ingredients will depend on the specific dish.

The common ingredients used for braising are:
>Beef—chuck, shank, brisket, short ribs, rounds, flanks, oxtail, heart, tongue
>Veal—shoulder, shank, breast, leg, sweetbreads, tongue, liver, heart
>Lamb—shoulder, shank, breast, sweetbreads
>Pork—shoulder, shank, hocks, ham, spare ribs

Common cooking liquids include:
>Stocks, beer, wine, marinades

There are three options for preparing the sauce:
1. After searing the product, deglaze the pan and add a light consistency brown sauce.
2. After searing the main product, add flour to the fat used to sear, and then add liquid.
3. After cooking the main product, reduce the cooking liquid and thicken.

In order to hold the braised item properly:
1. Hold large pieces in a small amount of stock to keep moist.
2. Keep the item covered.
3. Hold at a temperature above 135 degrees, but not so high as to dry the meat out.

There are some essential steps in the service of braised meat:
1. Carve large items against the grain.
2. A portion is three to four ounces (cooked weight).
3. Serve no more than two ounces of sauce per portion over the meat.

Remember:
1. The finished product must be tender but not stringy.
2. The finished sauce should be properly seasoned, balanced—not too much acid or vegetable flavor—and have a light consistency, not thick.

> **NOTE:**
> *Braising can make a tough cut of meat tender, flavorful, and profitable. Just look at the explosive popularity of short ribs over the past twenty years.*

Braising Procedure

Sear meat before simmering slowly in liquid and other ingredients.

Suitable for less-tender cuts of meat in larger portions: beef, veal, lamb, pork, game, poultry, seafood, and vegetables.

Remember:

-Use proper sized container.

-Cook meat properly so it is tender.

-Do not allow the meat to boil during cooking (causes the meat to shrink).

-Do not use too much liquid in the cooking container (causes the flavor of the sauce to weaken).

Equipment Needs:

      -Large pot

      -Tilt skillet

      -Roasting pan

Procedure:

1. Bone, trim, marinate, or season.
2. Dry the meat, then sear on all sides in a pot or tilt skillet.
3. Remove meat and add other ingredients.
4. Return meat to pot and bring to a simmer.
5. Cover and braise at a slow simmer in the oven or on stove top.
6. Check for doneness.
7. Remove the meat and finish the sauce.
8. Serve.

Classic Coq au Vin
Yield: 4 servings

Ingredients:
6 slices bacon, sliced into ½-inch pieces
8 chicken thighs
To taste: kosher salt
To taste: black pepper, freshly ground
1 onion, finely chopped
20 small pearl onions, peeled
½ cup shallots, minced (2 large shallots)
1 head garlic cloves separated and peeled
1 pound button mushrooms, wiped clean and halved (or quartered if large)
¼ cup all-purpose flour
2 teaspoons tomato paste
3 cups dry red wine
1½ cups rich chicken stock
6 sprigs fresh thyme or 1 teaspoon dried thyme
1 bay leaf
1 bunch parsley leaves, fresh

Preparation:
1. In a large, heavy Dutch oven over high heat, fry the bacon until crisp and all of the fat is rendered. Using a slotted spoon, transfer the crisp bacon bits to paper towels to drain.
2. Season the chicken pieces with the salt and pepper.
3. Brown the chicken pieces in the hot bacon fat, working in batches if necessary, and turning to ensure even cooking. Transfer the chicken pieces to a large plate or bowl and set aside. Remove some of the bacon fat, leaving about 4 tablespoons in the Dutch oven.
4. Reduce the heat to medium high and add the chopped onion, pearl onions, shallots, and garlic cloves to the Dutch oven and cook until soft, about 4 minutes.
5. Add the mushrooms and cook for 5 minutes longer, or until they've released most of their liquid and have begun to brown.
6. Add the flour and tomato paste. Cook, stirring constantly, for 1 minute.
7. Slowly add the wine and chicken stock, stirring constantly. Add the thyme, bay leaf, reserved bacon, and chicken.
8. Bring liquid to a boil. Cover the pot, place in a preheated (325ºF) oven, and cook for about ½ hour, or until the chicken is very tender.
9. Transfer the chicken pieces to a serving dish and cover loosely to keep warm.
10. Return pot to medium-low heat. Skim any fat from the surface of the cooking liquid and increase the heat to medium-high.
11. Cook until the sauce has thickened slightly and coats the back of a spoon, about 15–20 minutes.
12. Taste and adjust the seasoning if necessary.
13. Return the chicken to the Dutch oven and cook for a few minutes to heat through.
14. Plate, garnish with chopped parsley and serve.

REVIEW QUESTIONS

1. How does braising benefit less-tender cuts of meat?

2. Why must the pot used for braising have a tight-fitting lid?

3. Why might larding be necessary in the braising process?

4. Why is the meat dried?

5. How should the meat be placed in the oil?

6. Why should the liquid not be allowed to boil during the braising process?

7. Why should the meat be turned occasionally?

8. What is the process of degrassier?

9. What is the process of depouillage?

10. To thicken a sauce, what can be added?

11. How should a braised piece of meat be sliced?

12. Why is meat marinated?

13. How can you tell when the meat is done?

14. For every pound of meat, what amount of cooking liquid is required?

15. Name three common cooking liquids.

16. What are the three options for preparing the sauce?

17. What is the minimum holding temperature for the braised meat?

18. What is the proper way of holding the meat?

"The discovery of a new dish confers more happiness on humanity than the discovery of a new star."

J. A. Brillat-Savarin

5

BROIL AND GRILL

Definition

Considered two of the oldest forms of cooking, broiling and grilling require cooking close to a radiant heat or open flame.

Broiling means that the heat is applied from above, and in grilling the heat is applied from below.

These two dry-heat cooking methods are primarily used for *a la minute*, or cooked to order, items.

Grilling allows the drippings from the item to fall into the heat source, which turns them to smoke, giving the item that familiar smoky flavor.

Broiling is reserved for tender portion-sized pieces of meat, poultry, or fish. The heat is generated from above the item by an adjustable electric or gas source. Conduction heat from the broiler grates is minimal, though they do give the items the grill marks associated with this method of cooking.

Prepare the *mise en place*:
- Main item. chicken, pork, or steak
- Brine or marinade
- Salt, oil, pepper, other ingredients, and optional seasonings

The chicken must be cleaned and cut to its proper shape. Trim excess fat and skin.
1. Marinate the half chicken in a mixture of oil, salt, pepper, and seasonings.
2. When broiling the chicken, a hinged grill is used to assist in handling, retain shape, and limit sticking and tearing of the skin while broiling. Heat to full temperature; clean with a wire brush and oil the hinged grill.
3. Place the chicken skin side down and sear.
4. The broiler has a lever that controls the distance from the flame and the food. Place the hinged grill on the hottest place to mark the chicken. A visual check for a golden brown color, or "dore," will indicate when to turn the bird; this will then cook the chicken until done.
5. Care must be taken not to damage the skin.
6. The chicken can be placed in the oven to complete the cooking process.
7. The best check for doneness is a thermometer, unless you are very experienced.
8. Remember to monitor the cooking process to avoid overcooking the chicken.
9. Serve at once.

Method for Broiling a Steak:
1. Cuts of steak should be no more than two to three inches thick. Trim any excess fat to avoid flare-ups in the broiling process. Steaks may be marinated and can be brushed with oil before being placed on the grid.
2. The broiler is brought to full temperature, then cleaned with a wire brush and oiled.
3. Place the steak at an angle on the grids, and push the rack back into the broiler. Note: Safety must be a priority when broiling and grilling to avoid flash fires. Due to the high temperatures, any lack of atten- tion can be hazardous. A clean grill can cut down the potential for fires. In the case of a sudden flash

fire, the use of sheet pans or baking soda to extinguish the fire is effective. Be sure you know where the fire prevention devices are located.

4. After a short time, carefully check the steak with an offset-handled spatula. Check that the first grill marks are visible.

5. Rotate the item 180 degrees, to complete the pattern.

6. If the item is to be served immediately, continue with the cooking process. If it will be served at a later time, remove the steak and hold. If held, it must be undercooked and raised above its juices so that it does not continue to steam in its liquids.

7. At service time, the cooking process can be completed to the desired degree of doneness.

8. To determine doneness, the finger pressure method is the most valuable for the experienced griller. Firmness or resistance to pressure increases as the steak cooks toward well done.
   Visual methods can be unreliable, and a thermometer is highly recommended.

Method for Grilling:

Grills may use gas, charcoal, woods, or electricity. The food is exposed to radiant heat from below and to conductive heat that is transferred by the grids. The juices and fat rendered from the food fall to the heat source and create smoke, which enhances the flavor of the grilled item. The familiar criss-cross marking pattern is also associated with this method of cooking. The grill or broiler must be heated to full temperature to create these grill marks.

1. *Mise en place* should be conveniently located during this *a la minute* cooking method, and the grill should have temperature zones to regulate the different cooking stages. Some grills have adjustable grids to change the distance between the heat source and the food.
2. The grill must be heated to full temperature and cleaned and oiled between each item to avoid burned particles from adhering to the next item or allowing one flavor to affect another.
3. The food to be cooked should be prepared and ready to be placed on the grill soon after it has been oiled. Adequate ventilation is essential.

Mise en place **for grilling:**

   a. Main item, marinated
   b. Oil
   c. Seasonings

Method for grilling vegetables:

Common grilled vegetables are squash, peppers, and eggplant.

1. Wash the squash, leaving the skin on.
2. Cut thick slices at an angle to prevent the slices from drying out and to provide the greatest surface area.
3. Marinate the slices briefly in a combination of oil, salt, pepper, thyme, garlic, or marinade of your choice.
4. Once completely hot, prepare the grill by scraping off burned particles with a wire brush.
5. Oil the grill with a towel. Be sure there is proper ventilation.
6. When cooking vegetables, a moderate temperature is sufficient for marking and cooking without burning. Wipe off excess marinade and place the vegetables at an angle on the grill.
7. Visually check for the first set of marks by using an offset-handled spatula. Then turn the vegetables at an angle approximately 180 degrees.
8. When the second set of marks is visible, the item can be turned over to complete the cooking process.
9. Gently touch the item with your finger or the spatula to check for doneness.

Grilled vegetables should always be served immediately, as they do not retain their heat very well.

NOTE:

Grilling, broiling, and nutrition work well together. Broiled and grilled foods are very advantageous to a healthy diet due to the fact that many foods and fish have natural fat content that is rendered away from the intense heat and drips through the grates. This fat is lost; therefore, little fat is retained in the food as a result. Items that are poached and sautéed do not lose the fat, and therefore have more calories and sodium in the final product.

The grilling and broiling processes themselves impart a unique flavor at no nutritional cost, so additional garnishes and sauces may not be necessary. These sauces often add calories and sodium.

Grilling and broiling foods eliminate the need for these flavorings, and therefore they are very nutritious cooking methods. Flavor can be added to the food through the cooking method while remaining within nutrition guidelines. Grilling is suitable for healthy cooking if the method described above is followed.

Often, grilled foods are topped with a compound butter or other sauce, which may be emulsified with egg yolks or butter, thus countering the nutritional benefits of the grilled food.

There are three temperature zones in a broiler: high, medium, and low. The temperatures can range from 500-2,000°F.

Summary of Grilling and Broiling

Technique
Grilling uses dry high heat from the bottom.
A char grill uses an open flame.
A flat top grill is covered by a heavy metal top.
Broiling uses dry high heat from the top.

Suitable for tender meats with slight fat content, such as beef, veal, pork, chicken, and game, as well as seafood and vegetables.

Reminders
Cook thin items on high heat.
Start medium thick items on high heat and finish on the cooler part of the grill or broiler.
Start thick items on high heat and finish in the oven.
Grill/broil at the last moment prior to service.
Keep grill/broiler clean at all times.
Do not cook items too far ahead of time.
Do not pierce the meat while cooking (results in loss of juices).

Equipment Needs
Grill/broiler, gas or electric
Tongs and spatula
Grill thermometer
Grill cleaning items

Procedure:
Preheat grill or broiler.
Bone, trim, or portion item.
Season, marinate, and oil item.
Place item carefully on a clean grill.
Cook on both sides until proper degree of doneness is reached.
Serve immediately.

Pork Brine:

Yield: 5 cups

Brines have been used for centuries to preserve foods. This is a bullet-proof recipe to ensure a flavorful and moist chop or loin if followed exactly.

Ingredients:

5 cups water
¼ cup kosher salt
1.3 ounces sugar
5 thyme sprigs
1 garlic glove
1 tablespoon black pepper
1 teaspoon crushed red pepper
2 oranges, juice and zest

Preparation:

In a large saucepan, combine all ingredients and bring to a simmer.
Transfer to a bowl and let cool completely.
Add the pork and refrigerate for 24 hours. Be sure the meat is completely covered with brine.

Garlic-Citrus Marinade

Yield: ¾ cup

This is a delicious way to marinate skirt or flank steak as well as hangar steak, which lately has enjoyed growing popularity, and it's also good with chicken, pork, lamb, or vegetables.

Ingredients:

¼ cup fresh lime juice
¼ cup fresh orange juice
2 cloves garlic, minced
2 tablespoons olive oil
2 tablespoons red wine vinegar
2 tablespoons chopped fresh Italian parsley
1 teaspoon dried oregano

Preparation:

Place all the ingredients in a small jar with a tight-fitting lid.
Cover and shake to blend.
This marinade will keep in the refrigerator for up to 1 week.

Chimichurri Sauce

Yield: 2 cups

Argentinean restaurants often serve churrasco beef that is planked upright around a blazing fire. This recipe gives you much the same flavor, but in an easier preparation. The sauce, made with three different fresh herbs, along with garlic and sherry vinegar, makes a robust accompaniment to the gentle smokiness of the beef or other red meats.

Ingredients
½ cup fresh Italian parsley leaves
¼ cup fresh cilantro leaves
2 tablespoons fresh oregano leaves
½ cup sliced scallions
4 peeled garlic cloves
½ teaspoon cayenne pepper
½ teaspoon fine kosher or sea salt
½ teaspoon freshly ground black pepper
½ cup olive oil
½ cup sherry vinegar
¼ cup water—optional

Preparation:
In a food processor, combine all ingredients and process until smooth.

The sauce is best served the same day but will keep, in the refrigerator for up to five days.

REVIEW QUESTIONS

1. Briefly describe the broiling and grilling methods.

2. Is grilling or broiling appropriate for tough pieces of meat?

3. List the steps to broil a chicken half.

4. List the steps to broil a sirloin steak.

5. Why is high heat so important to the grilling and broiling process?

6. Why is a clean and oiled grill crucial to a well-grilled item?

7. What are two effective methods for extinguishing a grill fire?

8. Describe the test for doneness of broiled or grilled items.

9. Why is proper ventilation so important to the grilling and broiling cooking methods?

10. How is the grill markings created on a grilled item?

11. Can grilled vegetables be held for later service? Why or why not?

12. What are the three temperature zones for grilling?

13. Why is a wire brush an important part of the *mise en place* for grilling and broiling?

14. Why are broiling and grilling two cooking methods that are nutritious?

15. When grilling, if excess marinade is not wiped off, what will happen?

16. List the steps for grilling vegetables.

"If you know, recognize that you know. If you don't know, then realize that you don't know. That is knowledge."

Confucius

6

POACH AND STEAM

Definition

Poaching is a moist heat cooking method where the item is immersed into a liquid between 150ºF and 175ºF. The temperature is maintained throughout the cooking process with the liquid at a sparse bubble. The food item is gently cooked and does not dry out, making the poaching method highly suitable for fish and poultry. When one cuts into a poached piece of meat, it should be very moist, tender, and full of flavor. The taste should be very clean to the palate.

In shallow poaching, only a small amount of liquid is used and is later reduced and incorporated into a sauce.

The *mise en place* to shallow poaching is:

Protein, fish or chicken

Poaching medium, *fumet or* wine

Aromatics

Parchment paper

For the sauce:

Heavy cream

Herbs, chives, or parsley

Preparing the meat:

Timing, organization, and heat application are very important. Because of the thin nature of the food item, it's very important to have control of the application of heat in shallow poaching.

Using excessive heat will make the piece of meat undesirable, dry, and stringy.

1. The wine and *fumet* are placed into a sauté pan containing the aromatics and brought to a boil.
2. Once the poaching medium comes up to temperature, place the food item into the liquid.
3. Baste the food item with the liquid to ensure moistness. Cover it with paper and place it in a moderate oven.
4. Remove the fish from the oven and check for doneness. This can be done visually and by touch.
5. When done, plate the fish, recover it, and place it on the warming shelf, keeping it at serving temperature.

Preparing the sauce:

1. Return the sauté pan to the fire and reduce the poaching medium.
2. Strain the reduction into a saucepan and return it to the fire.
3. Check for consistency.
4. Add one ounce of double reduced cream and reduce it a little more.
5. Add the herbs at the last minute and the sauce is ready for plating.
6. Plate the sauce and arrange the meat on the plate.

Deep Poaching

Deep poaching entails placing the food item into a greater amount of liquid containing an acid, usually vinegar, which produces a firmer finished product.

Mise en place:
>Poaching medium
>Food item
>Salt and pepper

Procedure:
1. Place the poaching medium into the rondo and heat to just below the boiling point.
2. Remove the pan from the heat.
3. Introduce the food item, cover it, and return to a very low fire. Be careful that the poaching medium does not boil.
4. After about eight minutes, check for doneness by pressing on the food item with your finger.
5. Once it is done, remove the food item to the side to await plating.
6. Sauce the plate and place the fish on top of the sauce.

Putting the sauce underneath the fish shows off the excellence of the fish. At times, the fish may not appear as presentable. These are the times that you will want to sauce over the fish.

Mise en place **for deep poaching chicken:**
>Poaching medium
>Stock or *fumet*
>Chicken breast

For the sauce:
- Aromatics
- White wine
- *Fumet*
- Chives
- Tarragon
- Chervil
- Whipped cream

Preparation:
1. The chicken is deep poached using the same procedure as for the fish.
2. Once it is done, move the chicken to one side, plating it by slicing it diagonally most of the way through.
3. As in shallow poaching, the sauce is prepared from the reduction of wine and *fumet*, plus aromatics, *glace de volaille*, and double cream.
4. Add the herbs, stir a bit, and then add the whipped cream quickly. This will slow the cooking process, preventing the herbs from becoming too brown.
5. Sauce the plate and arrange the sliced chicken on top.

Steaming

Steaming is a moist cooking method in which a small amount of liquid is brought to and maintained at a boil. The level of the liquid is kept beneath the food item. The intensity of the boil determines the amount of steam. A hard boil will produce a more penetrating steam for larger, thicker food items, whereas a light boil will produce a steam that is less intense for smaller, more delicate items.

Steaming would be used instead of poaching when you don't lose the flavors and juices. When wanting to infuse a flavor into a piece of flesh, you would use poaching.

Mise en place for steaming fish:

> Steaming medium—*fumet*
> Fish

Mise en place for the sauce:

> Aromatics
> Wine
> *Fumet*
> Double cream
> Chives
> Whipped cream

Preparation:

1. Bring the steaming medium to a steady, even boil.
2. Introduce the fish directly into a steamer or into a vessel such as a shallow dish, and then into the steamer.
3. Cover and steam.
4. Check for doneness by pressing it with your finger—it should be resilient.
5. Once done, remove the fish to the side.

Prepare the sauce:

1. Sauté the shallots and bay leaf.
2. Add the white wine and the fumet and allow this mixture to reduce.
3. Strain the reduction into a small saucepan and continue to reduce, checking the sauce for consistency.
4. Stir in the double cream and reduce a little more.
5. At the last minute, add the chives and quickly mix in the whipped cream.
6. Sauce the plate.
7. Place the fish on top of the sauce.
8. Serve with appropriate starch and vegetable.

Poached Eggs Benedict
Yield: 4 servings

Ingredients:
Poached Eggs
3 quarts water, or as needed
2 teaspoons salt
6 tablespoons distilled white vinegar
8 large eggs
Eggs Benedict
8 slices Canadian bacon
8 poached eggs
4 English muffins split, toasted, and buttered
2 cups hollandaise sauce (separate recipe)

Preparation:

Poached Eggs:
1. Combine the water, salt, and vinegar in a deep pan and bring to a gentle simmer.
2. Break each egg into a clean cup, and carefully slide each egg into the poaching water.
3. Cook until the whites are set and opaque, about 3 minutes.
4. Remove the eggs from the water with a slotted spoon and blot them on absorbent toweling.
5. Serve immediately, or store chilled eggs in the refrigerator until needed.

Eggs Benedict:
1. Heat a sauté pan over medium-low heat.
2. Add the Canadian bacon and sauté on both sides until heated through, about 1–2 minutes on each side.
3. If eggs have been poached in advance, reheat them in simmering water until warmed through, and then remove with a skimmer.
4. Top each muffin half with a slice of Canadian bacon and a poached egg.
5. Spoon warm Hollandaise over each egg and serve.

Sauce Hollandaise
Yield: 12 servings

This is a great sauce to go with poached and steamed fish and vegetables, asparagus or cauliflower in particular.

Ingredients:
½ teaspoon cracked peppercorns
¼ cup white wine
¼ cup water, or as needed
4 large, fresh egg yolks
1½ cups butter, clarified, warm
2 teaspoons lemon juice, or as needed
2 teaspoons salt, or as needed
Pinch ground white pepper
Pinch cayenne

Preparation:
1. Combine the peppercorns and wine in a small pan and reduce over medium heat by half, about 5 minutes.
2. Add the water to the vinegar reduction. Strain this liquid into a stainless steel bowl.
3. Add the egg yolks to the reduction and set the bowl over a pot of simmering water.
4. Whisking constantly, cook the egg yolk and reduction until the yolks double in volume and become fluffy.
5. Remove the bowl from the simmering water and place it on a clean kitchen towel to keep the bowl from slipping.
6. Gradually add the warm butter into the egg mixture, whisking constantly. If the sauce becomes too thick and the butter is not blending in easily, add a little water to thin the egg mixture enough to whisk in the remaining butter.
7. Season the hollandaise sauce with lemon juice, salt, pepper, and cayenne (if desired).
8. Hold warm and serve within 2 hours.

DID YOU KNOW?

Sauces in French cuisine date back to the Middle Ages, when there were hundreds of sauces in the culinary repertoire. In the early nineteenth century, the chef Antonin Careme created an extensive list of sauces, many of which were original recipes. It is unknown how many sauces Carême is responsible for, but it is estimated to be in the hundreds. The cream sauce, in its most popular form around the world, was concurrently created by another chef, Dennis Leblanc, working in the same kitchen as Carême. In the late nineteenth century, Chef Auguste Escoffier consolidated Carême's list to five mother sauces:

1. Sauce Béchamel: milk-based sauce, thickened with a white roux.
2. Sauce Espagnole: a fortified brown veal stock sauce.
3. Sauce Velouté: white stock-based sauce, thickened with a roux or a liaison (a mixture of egg yolks and cream).
4. Sauce Hollandaise: an emulsion of egg yolk, butter, and lemon or vinegar.
5. Sauce Tomate: tomato-based.

"Sauces are the splendor and the glory of French cooking."

Julia Child

REVIEW QUESTIONS

1. What type of cooking method is poaching?

2. How much liquid is used in shallow poaching?

3. What will excessive heat do to a piece of meat in the poaching process?

4. How can doneness of a food item be checked?

5. Why would deep poaching be used instead of shallow poaching?

6. Where should the sauce be placed when plating the food item?

7. What type of cooking method is steaming?

8. During steaming, is the liquid brought to a boil?

9. Where should the level of the liquid be kept during steaming?

10. During steaming, when should a hard boil be used?

11. When would one use steaming instead of poaching?

12. If one wanted to infuse flavor into a food item, would steaming or poaching be used?

"Let food be thy medicine, and medicine be thy food."

Hippocrates

7

BOIL AND BLANCH

Definition
Boiling is a wet cooking method utilizing water or another water-based liquid, such as stock or milk. Boiling is a very harsh technique of cooking, unlike simmering or poaching. Delicate foods such as fish cannot be cooked in this fashion because the bubbles can damage the food. Foods such as red meat, chicken, and root vegetables can be cooked with this technique because of their tough texture.

There are five basic stages to the boiling technique:
1.   Bring the liquid to a full boil and add seasonings or aromatics.
2.   Add the vegetable to the liquid.
3.   Cook to the desired doneness.
4.   Drain or remove the item.
5.   Serve immediately or refresh and hold for later service.

Boiling is comprised of three elements:
The product
Cooking medium
Seasonings and aromatics

The product:
An item to be boiled needs to be of the highest quality, must be as fresh as possible, and needs to be prepared for boiling. The fresh vegetable is cut and sized for cooking. Uniformity of size is important to make sure that the vegetable cooks evenly. The cut is usually determined by its final use and plate appearance. Broccoli used as a side dish may be cut into even flowerets. Carrots could be sliced, julienned, or tourned. Other vegetables may be diced, while a few are commonly cooked whole.
Whenever possible, one should make use of excess trimmings. They are suitable for use in soups, stir-fries, or purees. Unusable trim should be disposed of properly.
Composting is recommended for unusable trim. Uniformity of size is essential for even cooking.
Product quality is essential, as it affects your yield and productivity. Once the vegetables are prepared, they will move into production for current and future use. Organization and planning ahead are critical for success.
Menu planning must occur in advance to allow for purchasing of the best quality products. This will allow scheduling and production to be efficient. Working in teams using organized systems is very useful.

The cooking medium:
Water is the most commonly used liquid, but you may use stocks and *court bouillon* to add a desired flavor to the finished dish.
The amount of liquid will depend upon the vegetable and the required cooking time. The quantity to be cooked will also factor in the production method.

It is recommended that you cook only what you need, in the shortest amount of cooking time. The liquid should be able to hold the vegetable comfortably, without excess crowding.

The cooking medium is brought to a full rolling boil. Covering the pot will bring the liquid to a boil more quickly. You may want to add salt to the liquid, but use only enough to make the taste barely apparent.

The liquid must be at a full boil before adding the product. There are a few exceptions to this, when the product is added to the water before boiling. An example of this is beets, because of their density when cooked whole before peeling.

Artichokes and leeks are cooked in *court bouillon*; cauliflower in water with milk to keep the white color.

Acids, such as vinegar or wine, are commonly added to the cooking medium to set the color of red vegetables.

Seasonings and Aromatics

Seasonings, salt, pepper, and aromatics are used to impart additional flavor to the boiled item. They can be added to the cooking liquid or may be combined with the vegetable once it has boiled.

Acidic ingredients such as wine or vinegar are added to the cooking medium to achieve a desired flavor. Use these with caution. You might cause green beans to turn gray, or broccoli to turn yellow.

Aromatics such as star anise or allspice berries can infuse a flavor during the cooking process to compliment the natural flavor.

Tossing with herbs, olive oil, or butter is a common way to finish boiled vegetables.

Boiling Procedure:

1. Cooking medium must be at a full boil.
2. The product is added in small batches so that the water never stops boiling. A medium rolling boil should be maintained. A vigorous boil might damage the vegetables.
3. Covering the pot will depend on the type of vegetable being cooked. Green vegetables should not be covered because the lid will capture and contain the natural acids that will turn them to an undesirable dull olive or yellow-green color. Some red and white vegetables will actually retain and enhance their color if the acids are trapped. Covering the pot may exaggerate strong flavors and aromas, but in most cases covering the pot will merely speed up cooking time.

When cooking vegetables like beans, cauliflower, and carrots:

Just prior to service, the vegetables are cooked for approximately four minutes. They are placed in a "wash" of whole butter or olive oil.

You may add Vietnamese fish sauce, which lends a salty flavor to the vegetable; then the vegetable is ready for service. Continue cooking the vegetable, periodically checking for doneness. Each vegetable has an expected average cooking time. As this time approaches, use a slotted spoon to remove a test piece and check for doneness.

As you cut into this piece, be aware of its firmness and resiliency. You can see and feel the doneness, regardless of the type of vegetable. This sense is acquired through experience and can be invaluable in vegetable cookery.

A vegetable is not acceptable if it is overcooked or undercooked. Allow the vegetable to cool briefly, and taste. The vegetable should not be too crispy or mushy. It should have the appropriate flavor and tenderness.

This test evaluation is essential to know the quality of your final product, and to be sure your customer is served only the best. When vegetables have reached the proper doneness, drain them thoroughly with a colander or sieve, or remove them with a slotted spoon. The vegetable should be served immediately—as is, or topped with butter, fresh herbs, or spices. Or it can be served with an optional sauce.

Variations of Boiling

Two variations often used are blanching or parboiling. Parboiling is sometimes known as par cooking.

Blanching:

Blanching can be used to make the skins of tomatoes easy to remove; to eliminate or reduce strong odors or flavors; to set the color of vegetables to be served cold, or as a first step to other preparations, such as pan-fried zucchini or a sauté of mixed vegetables.

Blanching vegetables can equalize the final process times of different items, giving you more control at service time.

To blanch the vegetable, it is very briefly boiled. This affects only the outer surface, and barely begins the cooking process. It is essential to keep the cooking time as brief as possible. The vegetable is shocked immediately in an ice water bath to stop the cooking process.

Parboiling:

Parboiling is similar to blanching, taking the cooking process a bit further. The item is cooked for a slightly longer time, although the vegetable is still not fully cooked.

Parboiled vegetables are more resistant in firmness than fully boiled vegetables. This shortens the cooking time of the vegetables that may be used in another preparation, such as braising, grilling, or gratins.

Parboiling is commonly used in kitchens to prepare pastas and potatoes, but works just as well with vegetables.

Summary

Vegetables are a healthy food valued for their wide range of flavors, bright colors, and versatility. For these reasons and more, vegetables have a firmly established place on the contemporary menu.

The universal technique of boiling can be very simple when the basics are understood.

Five stages of boiling:

1. Bring the liquid to a full boil. Add seasonings or aromatics.
2. Add the vegetables to the liquid.
3. Cook until the vegetable has reached the desired doneness.
4. Drain or remove the item from the liquid.
5. Serve immediately, or refresh and hold for later use.

Practical experience is invaluable when cooking vegetables in order to know what specific steps to take and know how to determine proper doneness. Vegetables are as versatile as the chef who prepares them.

They offer so much to a meal in color, flavor, and nutrition, whether served as a side dish or main course.

DID YOU KNOW?

Cereals
Maize, wheat, and rice together account for 87 percent of all grain production worldwide and 43 percent of all food calories, while the production of oats and rye has drastically fallen from their 1960s levels.
Barley and sorghum follow the ranking list.
Teff, an ancient grain, is a staple in Ethiopia but scarcely known elsewhere. It is high in fiber and protein. Its flour is often used to make *injerea*, a yeast-risen flat bread, but it can also be eaten as a warm breakfast cereal with a chocolate or nutty flavor.
Amaranth, an ancient staple crop of the Aztecs, is now widely grown in Africa.

Hard-Boiled Eggs
Yield: 4 eggs

When we speak of eggs, we're generally talking about the eggs that come from chickens. Without eggs, the culinary arts as we know them wouldn't exist. Eggs are a crucial ingredient in all sorts of culinary preparations, from baked goods to sauces. They're also one of the most nutritious and versatile foods in their own right.

Ingredients:
4 large eggs
Water, as needed

Preparation:
1. Place eggs in a heavy-bottomed saucepan and cover them with cold water.
2. Make sure the tops of the eggs are covered by at least 1 inch of water. How much water will depend on the size of the pot, but generally a larger pot is better. Crowding the eggs risks cracking them.
3. Bring the water to a full boil, uncovered. Remove the pot from the heat and cover it.
4. Let the pot stand untouched for 17 minutes.
5. Remove the boiled eggs from the water and transfer them to a bowl of cold water. Let the eggs sit for 15 minutes.
6. Peel and serve the eggs, or refrigerate them.

> **NOTE:**
> *One thing to know about properly hard-boiled eggs is that you should never see a greenish ring around the yolk when it's cut it open. The sulfur in the egg causes the green discoloration when the egg has been boiled for too long and becomes overheated, meaning the egg has been overcooked. By using the technique mentioned above, you can say good-bye to those greenish, overcooked egg yolks.*

DID YOU KNOW?

When boiled eggs are hard to peel, it's an indication of the eggs' freshness, not a reflection as to how it was cooked. Fresher eggs will be harder to peel; older eggs are easier to peel. So if you have some older eggs in your fridge, those would be a better choice for making hard-boiled eggs than ones you just grabbed from the henhouse.

Ever wondered about the difference between brown-shelled eggs and white ones? Nutritionally speaking, they are the same. The only difference between these two eggs is that they are laid by different breeds of hens.

Egg Sizes:

Egg sizes are determined by weight. Large eggs, which weigh an average of two ounces each, are standard, so use large eggs when a recipe doesn't specify the size.

The minimum weights per dozen for each size are:

Jumbo	30 ounces
Extra Large	27 ounces
Large	24 ounces
Medium	21 ounces
Small	18 ounces
Pee Wee	15 ounces

Grading Eggs:

Grades AA and A are the only grades that are generally sold to the public. The difference between the two grades is mainly a function of age. The older an egg, the more it spreads out when broken, the thinner the white is, and the flatter the yolk stands.

Egg Storage:

As long as eggs are kept refrigerated, you can use them up to four weeks past their "sell-by" date. However, once eggs are out of their shells, they should be used within a couple of days. Egg shells are quite porous, and strong smells can seep into them. Eggs should be kept in their cartons rather than in the built-in egg shelves inside of some refrigerators.

Egg Freshness:

Inside every egg is an air pocket. Because of its porous shell, air passes through it over time, causing this air pocket to expand. Therefore, you can determine an egg's freshness by its buoyancy by placing it in a glass of water.

If the egg sinks and lies flat on the bottom, it's pretty fresh. An egg that is a week old should just begin to float. At three weeks, the egg may stand upright at the bottom of the glass. If an egg floats to the surface, it shouldn't be used. This "spread test" can also be useful when checking the freshness of an egg.

Egg Safety:

Raw eggs contain the salmonella bacteria, which can lead to a food-borne illness. Wash your hands thoroughly when you handle raw eggs, and make sure your eggs are cooked thoroughly. For preparations that contain uncooked egg (such as mayonnaise), pasteurized eggs should be used. Pasteurized eggs have been treated with heat to eliminate salmonella.

Egg Nutrition:

Eggs are a nearly complete source of nutrition and are rich in protein and iron. They also supply vitamins A, D, E, K, and B-complex. The egg white is fat free and high in protein. In the past, eggs were thought to be unhealthy due to their cholesterol content. Today, nutritionists agree that the cholesterol in eggs is the "good" kind.

One large egg contains:

Calories	75
Cholesterol	215 milligrams, in the yolk
Protein	6 grams

REVIEW QUESTIONS

1. What are the three elements of boiling?

2. Why is it important that vegetables are cut into a uniform size and shape prior to boiling?

3. What can be done with the excess trimmings from vegetables?

4. List two common mediums for cooking vegetables.

5. When the cooking medium is brought to a full boil, should you put all of the vegetables in at once? Why or why not?

6. What technique is used to set the white color of cauliflower?

7. Acids may be added to the cooking medium for what color of vegetables? Why is this helpful?

8. What are some examples of the optional components of the boiling method?

9. What will happen to a green vegetable, such as broccoli, if vinegar or wine is added to the cooking medium?

10. True or false: All vegetables should be covered during the cooking process. Explain your answer.

11. Explain the procedure to test for doneness in vegetables.

12. How does blanching differ from boiling?

13. When might you blanch a vegetable, rather than boil it?

14. How does parboiling differ from blanching?

15. If green vegetables are covered during the cooking process, what will occur?

16. Is it necessary to cut all vegetables prior to boiling? Why or why not?

"Tell me what you eat, and I will tell you what you are."

J. A. Brillat-Savarin, 1755–1826

8

STOCKS

Definition

White stock, brown stock, and *fumet* (essence) are the three basic stocks used. Traditionally a stock is made by simmering various ingredients in water. Given the importance of stock and its relationship to so many other areas of the culinary arts, it's worth taking the time to understand the purpose of each ingredient and the properties each one brings to the stock.

Meat

Leftover cooked meat, such as that remaining on poultry carcasses, is often used along with the bones of the bird, or joints. Fresh meat makes a superior stock, and cuts rich in connective tissue, such as shin or shoulder of beef or veal, are commonly recommended, either alone or added in lower proportions to the remains of cooked poultry to provide a richer and fresher-tasting stock.

Quantities recommended are in the ratio of one part fresh meat to two parts water.

Pork is considered unsuitable for stock in European cooking due to its greasiness (although nineteenth-century recipes for consommé and traditional aspic included ham).

Bones

Veal, beef, and chicken bones are most commonly used. The flavor of the stock comes from the cartilage and connective tissue in the bones. Connective tissue has collagen in it, which gets converted into gelatin that thickens the liquid. Stock made from bones needs to be simmered for longer than stock made from meat. Pressure cooking methods shorten the time necessary to extract the flavor from the bones.

Mirepoix

Mirepoix is a combination of onions, carrots, celery, and sometimes other vegetables. Often, the less desirable parts of the vegetables (those that may not otherwise be eaten, such as carrot skins and celery ends) are used. The use of these parts is highly dependent upon the chef, as many do not appreciate the flavors that these portions impart.

Herbs and spices

The herbs and spices used depend on availability and local traditions. In classical cuisine, the use of a *bouquet garni* consisting of parsley, bay leaves, a sprig of thyme, and possibly other herbs, is common. This is often placed in a sachet to make it easier to remove once the stock is cooked.

Stock vs. broth

The procedure for making white stock differs from that of brown stock, mainly in that rather than roasting the bones beforehand, they are blanched instead. Blanching helps get rid of the impurities in the bones that can cloud the stock.

Note that a white stock can be made using chicken bones, veal bones, or beef bones.

The difference between broth and stock is one of both cultural and colloquial terminology, but certain definitions prevail. Stock is the thin liquid produced by simmering raw ingredients; solids are removed, leaving a thin, highly flavored liquid. This gives a classic stock as made from beef, veal, chicken, fish, and vegetables.

Broth differs in that it is a basic soup where the solid pieces of flavoring—meat or fish, along with some vegetables—remain.

DID YOU KNOW?

Remouillage is a second stock made from the same set of bones

Dashi stock, used in Japanese cooking, is made from kelp and fermented bonito. It is the base for miso soup, clear broth, noodle broth, and many kinds of simmering liquid.

Chicken Stock Recipe
Yield: 1 gallon

Chicken stock is incredibly versatile. You can use it as a base for soups and sauces, a cooking liquid for rice or risotto, for braising poultry or vegetables, and so on. A few tips:
- The neck, back, ribs, and wings are excellent for making chicken stock. Best of all, however, are the feet.
- Always start with cold water. This helps extract more collagen, giving the stock more body.
- Don't let the stock boil. It should stay at a gentle simmer.
- Don't stir the stock as it simmers! All you need to do while it simmers is skim the scum off the top, and add water if it drops too low.

Ingredients
For Sachet:
- 1 bay leaf
- ½ teaspoon dried thyme
- 3–4 fresh parsley stems
- 3–4 whole black peppercorns
- 1 whole clove

Stock
- 2–3 pounds chicken bones (or the carcass from a roasted chicken)
- 1 medium onion, peeled and chopped
- 1 medium rib celery, chopped
- 1 medium carrot, peeled and chopped

Preparation:
1. Make a *sachet d'epices* by tying the bay leaf, thyme, parsley stems, peppercorns, and clove into a piece of cheesecloth.
2. Rinse chicken bones in cold water and transfer to a heavy-bottomed stockpot.
3. Add enough cold water to the pot to completely cover the bones—about 5 quarts.
4. Bring pot to a boil, then immediately drain and rinse bones.
5. Return the blanched bones to the pot and again cover with fresh, cold water.
6. Bring pot to a boil, and then lower the heat to a simmer.
7. Skim off the scum that rises to the surface.
8. Add *mirepoix* (chopped onion, celery, and carrots) to the pot along with the sachet; tie the sachet string to the stockpot handle for easy retrieval later.
9. Simmer for about 4 hours, continuing to skim the impurities that rise to the surface. Liquid will evaporate, so make sure there's always enough water to cover the bones.
10. After 4 hours, remove from the heat and strain the stock through a sieve lined with a few layers of cheesecloth.
11. Cool the stock quickly, using an ice bath if necessary
12. Label, date, and store.

Fish Stock Recipe
Yield: 1 gallon

Fish stock or *fumét* as it's called in French, is quick and easy to make and is a really magnificent base for fish soups, chowders, seafood risotto, any number of sauces, and many other uses.The best fish bones to use are those from mild, lean, white fish like halibut, cod, or flounder. Fish to avoid are salmon, trout, mackerel, or other oily, fatty fish.

Ingredients
For Sachet:
- 2–3 whole peppercorns
- 3–4 parsley stems
- ½ bay leaf
- 1 whole clove
- 1 pinch dried thyme

Stock
- 2 tablespoons butter
- 1 medium rib celery, chopped
- 1 medium carrot, peeled and chopped
- 1 medium onion, peeled and chopped
- 4 pounds fish bones (see note), with heads; remove gills
- 1 cup dry white wine
- 1 gallon cold water

Preparation:
1. Make a *sachet d'epices* by tying the peppercorns, parsley stems, bay leaf, clove, and thyme into a piece of cheesecloth.
2. In a heavy-bottomed stock pot or soup pot, heat the butter over medium heat.
3. Lower the heat; add the vegetables and sweat, with the lid on, for about 5 minutes or until the onions are softened and slightly translucent. Don't brown the vegetables, though.
4. Add the fish bones and sweat for another couple of minutes, covered, until the bones are slightly opaque.
5. Add the wine and bring up the heat until it starts to simmer. Then add the sachet and the water, heat to a simmer, and let simmer for 30–45 minutes.
6. Strain (remove fish bones first if that makes it easier), cool, and refrigerate.

Bouquet Garni
A bundle of herbs and aromatics tied within sections of leek with cooking twine and simmered in stock to add flavor and aroma. In addition to leeks, components are celery, thyme, parsley stems, and bay leaf.

DID YOU KNOW?

Sachet d'épices translates literally to "bag of spices" in French.

Step By Step Chicken Stock Preparation

1, Butcher the chicken,
    choose the bones

 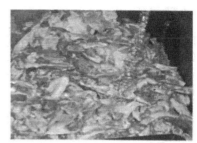

2, Rinse, add water and bring to a boil
    8 pound bones
    6 quarts water

3, Decrease and simmer for 2 hours

4, Add spice bag and simmer

5, Add mire poix
    1 pound mire poix

6, Simmer another hour

7. Strain and cool

8, Label, date and store

Brown Stock

The procedure for making brown stock differs from that of white stock mainly in that instead of blanching the bones beforehand, they are roasted instead. Roasting bones and *mirepoix* brings out more color and flavor. Also, some sort of tomato product is used with brown stocks, again for adding color and flavor, but also because the acid in the tomato helps dissolve the connective tissues in the bones, thus aiding in the formation of gelatin.

Bones for Making Stock:

Bones contain *collagen*, which, when simmered, forms *gelatin*. The more gelatin there is in the stock, the more body it will have. When chilled, a good stock should actually solidify.

Types of bones that are naturally high in cartilage include:

- So-called "knuckle bones" found in the large joints.
- Bones of younger animals, which is why veal bones are so desirable.

White Stock vs. Brown Stock:

White stocks are used as the base for *velouté* sauce and various derivative sauces, such as the *allemande* and *supreme* sauces.

Brown stocks are used for making *demiglace* and its derivatives, such as *bordelaise* and Robert.Note that beef or veal bones can be used for either white or brown stocks. The difference is that when making white stock, the bones are blanched first, or quickly boiled, then drained and rinsed before simmering.

For brown stock, the bones are roasted before simmering, and some sort of tomato product is usually added. The roasting and tomato product give the brown stock its darker color.

Use Cold Water for Making Stock:

The reason we start with *cold* water is that certain proteins, notably *albumin*, will only dissolve in cold water. And albumin helps clarify a stock. Therefore, starting with cold water results in a clearer stock. Speaking of water, much of the process of making stock comes down to removing impurities. You want to start with the purest water you can get; use filtered water whenever possible.

Aromatic Vegetables for Stock (*Mirepoix*):

Mirepoix is a combination of chopped carrots, celery, and onions used to add flavor and aroma to stocks. The usual proportions (by weight) for making *mirepoix* are:

- 50 percent onions, 25 percent carrots, and 25 percent celery

How Acid Affects Stock:

Acid helps break down the cartilage and other connective tissues in the bones, thus accelerating the formation of gelatin. The acid products used are generally one or another of the following:

- **Tomato:** Brown stocks use some sort of tomato product, usually tomato paste, which also adds color and flavor to the stock.
- **Wine:** White stock and chicken stock sometimes use white wine, and fish stock almost always does.

Remember: Acid reacts with aluminum cookware, so use a stainless steel stockpot for making stock.

Flavorings and Aromatics:
Small amounts of herbs, spices, and additional aromatics can be added to stock, using one of two methods:
Sachet d'epices: a small cheesecloth sack of dried and fresh herbs and spices.
Bouquet garni: a bundle of herbs and aromatics tied within sections of leek with cooking twine.
Both are simmered in the stock at the end of a cooking twine tied to the handle of the stockpot, making it easy to retrieve.

Seasoning Stock:
Because stock is often further reduced, it's better to season your sauces just before service time rather than salting your stock.

Preparing Brown Stock
1. Place the bones in the pan and place in the oven for browning at 400 degrees. Visually, you may see some of the haze coming out of the pan.
2. Turn the bones. This should be done as quickly as possible to avoid losing heat from the oven.
3. Once the sizzling of the bones has been achieved, turn the heat down. The bones should achieve a rich, golden brown, or "dore" color. Avoid over roasting the bones because it will render a stock that is too dark and it will impact the flavor.
4. Remove the bones with a skimmer; leave the fat and oil behind. You do not want fats or oils in your stock. The stockpot being used should be tall, with narrow sides and a small surface. Do not use one that is short and has a wide surface. When you skim the impurities that will rise in the initial stages of the cooking process, you can easily remove them if you are using a tall and narrow pot. Also, with a tall and narrow pot, you will have the least amount of evaporation because you will have better control of the cooking process.
5. Cut the vegetable for the *mirepoix*. Celery is not added at this point because its high moisture content inhibits caramelization and browning.
6. The *mirepoix*, minus the celery, is placed in the conditioned pan at this point.
7. Work quick and neatly, and transfer the vegetables for the *mirepoix* into the pan using a pan, not your hands. The *mirepoix* should be sizzling and the vegetables should be caramelizing. This means that the natural sugars in the vegetables are cooking and turning a rich brown color.
8. In the pan, a crust will have adhered to the bottom of the pan as a result of roasting the bones. This is called the fond. During the caramelization process, this fond will be released when the vegetables are stirred.
9. Add a little tomato paste for flavor and color, and fry it with the *mirepoix* and the fat. Do not allow the tomato paste to burn or blacken. Stir. The aroma of the vegetables should be fragrant.
10. Deglaze the pan with water; this loosens any remaining bits of the fond. A small amount of water is sufficient to do this. The color of the liquid at this point will not be dark, but a brownish color. When the deglazing process is finished, remove the bones.

Cooking the stock:
1. Pour the water approximately three inches over the bones in the stockpot. Place the pot on high heat and allow it to come to a boil. Simmer it at a slow, "lazy bubble" for at least three hours.
2. Skim the impurities as they accumulate on the surface.
3. The *sachet d'epices* has aromatics in it: peppercorns, parsley stems, bay leaf, thyme, and garlic. Herbs and spices for the sachet can vary. When using dried spices and herbs, a maximum of one hour will allow for the optimum extraction of flavor. If it is allowed to remain in the stock for too long, the flavors will dull. It is added at the latter portion of cooking the stock.
4. After the stock has simmered for approximately three hours, add the *mirepoix* and the celery to the stockpot. The stock should cook at a slow, "lazy bubble." This will allow the stock to remain clear. If the boil is too fast, the fat that has risen to the top of the stock will be forced back into it, creating a cloudy stock.

Straining, Cooling, and Storing the Stock:

1. Strain the stock with a china cap and cheesecloth. The cheesecloth should be moistened with plain cold water to prevent it from slipping in the china cap as the stock is being poured over it. Moistened cheesecloth will cling to the china cap.

2. To cool the stock, place a rack in the bottom of the sink to create space between the bottom of the pot and the sink. This will allow cold ice water to get underneath the pot.

3. Pour ice and cold water into the sink. The water must come up to the level of the stock to ensure proper cooling. As the stock cools, it will be rotated in the sink to help the cooling process. Note that the stock is being cooled in a stainless steel container. Plastic cannot be used at this stage because it will not release heat as well as the metal.

4. Alternatively you can chill the stock in the A-S-Quick chiller.

5. After the stock is cold, transfer it to a plastic container for storage.

6. Cover, label, and date the stock.

7. This will ensure that stocks can be properly rotated and used according to date made. Stocks must be used within two to three days.

Review for Brown Stock:

1. *Mise en place*, including bones, ingredients for *mirepoix*, the *sachet d'epices*, and kitchen equipment.
2. Condition the pan.
3. Place bones in the pan and brown in the oven until golden brown, or "dore." Utilize your senses (sight and smell) to determine when the bones are done.
4. Chop the onions and carrots and place them in the conditioned pan. Add tomato paste. Deglaze the pan.
5. Cover the bones in the stockpot with enough water to cover them by at least three inches.
6. Bring to a boil. Simmer for three hours at a slow, lazy bubble. Add *mirepoix* and simmer three additional hours. Remove impurities with ladle and napkin during the simmering process. Add the sachet for the last hour of simmering.
7. Strain, cool, and store for no more than three days.

REVIEW QUESTIONS

1. List the ingredients for brown stock.

2. What types of bones are best suited for brown stock?

3. List the equipment needed for making stocks.

4. What is a *sachet d'epices*? What is it used for?

5. What type of stockpot is best suited for making stocks? Why?

6. When making brown stock, the onions and carrots of the *mirepoix* are added first. Why is the celery added later in the process?

7. True or false: All stocks should cook at a rapid boil. Explain.

8. Explain the procedure for straining a stock.

9. Explain the procedure to cool stocks. Why is cooling done in this manner?

10. List the steps for making brown stock.

11. How long are the following stocks cooked?

    Veal____Beef____Chicken____

12. What is the recommended ratio of bones, water, and *mirepoix* for one gallon of white stock?

13. List the steps for making white stock.

14. What are the four components of fish stock?

15. What types of bones are best suited for fish stock?

16. What are some items used for stocks (list three)?

DID YOU KNOW?

Veal bones are cooked for about six hours.
Beef bones are cooked for about eight hours.
Chicken bones are cooked for about three hours.

The ratio for one gallon stock:
8 pounds bones
6 quarts water
1 pound *mirepoix*
Neutral flavor

What is fond?
Fond is the French word for stock. It is also the name for the little roasty bits left at the bottom of a pan where something has been cooked. From the French word for "bottom," *fond* is the word for those little roasty bits.

"*Everyone eats and drinks; yet only few appreciate the taste of food.*"

Confucius

9

ROAST

Definition

Roasting and baking are very similar in that they are dry cooking methods that utilize dry heated air surrounding the food to cook it in an oven. Their primary difference lies in the fact that roasting applies to proteins, whereas baking generally applies to vegetables, starches, breads, and pastries. In principle, roasting meats is a simple procedure. The prepared cut of meat is placed in an oven at a selected temperature and removed when it is done. There are many variables on the finer points of roasting, and chefs often disagree about proper roasting techniques. In this section we will discuss the basic steps for roasting.

Prepare the *mise en place*
- Main item: meat, fish, poultry, vegetables, or fruit
- Barding/larding or other flavoring/moisturizing ingredients
- Stuffing's, coatings, crusts, and seasoning mixtures
- Stock or brown sauce, including other items as required

Select cuts from legs and/or loins for the best results. Poultry and fowls should be roasted whole for best results. Traditionally the skin on poultry items is allowed to remain. While the fat renders, a natural basting process occurs. *Barding/ larding* allows you to add moisture to cuts that have little inherent fat.

1. Prepare the necessary equipment. Roasting pans and baking sheets should be of the proper size, large enough to allow for proper air circulation but not so large that the rendered juices and fat will scorch. The more air the product receives, the better the roasting process. For this reason, racks, *mirepoix,* and even bones are used to elevate the meat and allow airflow. Steam should be avoided as it can toughen the finished product, so roast uncovered.
2. Trim the fat and season the items. Fatty items should be trimmed to about one-half inch. Roasts should be seasoned with the desired combinations of herbs and spices. This can be done well ahead to allow the flavors to penetrate.
3. Searing is the initial step for some roasted products. It seals in the juices and allows for a juicier end product. Searing is normally done with a small amount of fat on the flat-top or stove top for smaller, more manageable items. Larger items may be seared, starting the roasting process at a very high temperature and then scaling back the temperature for the remainder of cooking.
4. Place items to be roasted fat side up in the roasting pan and cook, while monitoring time and temperature. This cooking continues until you reach a desired degree of doneness. Larger roasts are usually cooked at a low to moderate temperature, while smaller roasts are cooked at a higher temperature, allowing surface color to develop in relation to the shorter time needed for cooking.
5. Basting is recommended by using melted fats rendered from the food item and poured over the item by spoon, ladle, or brush. This helps caramelize the surface and add flavor. No external moisture should be added.

Mirepoix is used during the roasting process to contribute flavor to the natural jus or gravies derived from the drippings. The rate in which the *mirepoix* is caramelized depends on the cut of the vegetables as well as the cooking time and temperature. To keep it from burning, it should be added thirty to forty minutes before the roast is due to be removed from the oven. It can also be finished in a pan after the roast is removed.

The degree of doneness refers to the item's desired internal temperature. This can be determined by several methods:

1. If a thermometer is used, make sure it is kept away from any bone or fat pocket, which will interfere with an accurate reading. This is the most accurate method.
2. Another practical method is to use a metal skewer. First, pierce the meat with a long skewer or needle to the center of the muscle. Then remove it and touch it to a sensitive area, such as below your lip or to your forearm. It will feel lukewarm it the item is rare to medium rare. Note: awareness of sanitary standards is important here.
3. The finger pressure method is also learned by experience to sense the right amount of resistance. If the item is rare, it is soft. Medium is a little firmer, and well done is firm.

Roasts must be removed from the oven before the desired internal temperature is reached because carryover cooking continues within the cut. It should be removed five to fifteen degrees before the desired temperature is reached, depending on size.

The roast should be carefully removed from the pan with a kitchen fork or spatula. It should have a resting period of twenty to thirty minutes. During this time, carryover cooking will continue and juices that have concentrated in the center will redistribute uniformly as the muscle begins to relax. The roast will carve nicely and bleeding of the juices will be minimized. The cut should be held uncovered at a warm temperature that reflects the principles of kitchen sanitation. The item cannot be held under 140 degrees. The meat should not be carved until service time. The item can rest standing up to prevent juices from running out of the roast.

Poultry

1. When roasting poultry, it is necessary to truss or tie the item. This will improve shape and allow for uniform cooking. To tie poultry, string is used to wrap around the tail, neck, legs, and wings. Tying styles differ from chef to chef.
2. Another method is to truss the item with needle and string. This is done by passing the needle through one leg, into the back, and through the other leg. The string enters the wing, goes through the neck, through the other wing, and is returned to the original leg, where it is double knotted.
3. Brushing the poultry with butter or oil before seasoning will reduce blistering of the skin and allow for more browning. Seasoning is suggested at this time.
4. Small poultry, such as quails and hens, can be seared on the stove. Close attention should be paid to not damage the skin. Caramelization can be achieved in the oven with basting and proper temperature, eliminating the need to sear the item.
5. The item is placed in an appropriately sized pan just large enough to hold the item. The use of a rack is recommended for fattier poultry such as goose or duck.
6. The poultry is then placed in a preheated oven. The roasting time depends on the size of the item.
7. Basting is required for most poultry items by using melted fats extruded from the item. This will give the roast an attractive brown outer surface.
   Note: Each time the oven is opened, you are losing heat.
8. *Mirepoix* is added during the latter part of the roasting process, enhancing the flavor of the basting liquid. For items such as roasted quail, *mirepoix* can be added at the beginning of the roasting process or sautéed separately before being cooked along with the roast.
9. To check for doneness, various methods can be used:
   a   A thermometer.
   b   The finger pressure method.

c   Twist the leg of the item to check the firmness of the joint.

d   The poultry can also be raised and a fork can be inserted into the cavity, allowing the juices to run out into a pan or a plate, checking to see if there is an absence of a red or rosy color (referred to as "juices that run clear").

Small poultry should be served immediately instead of allowing a resting period as is done for larger roasts. The drippings left in the pan are comprised of juices, *fond*, and fat. The *fond* is the caramelization of the drippings and can form on the bottom of the pan and also adhere to the *mirepoix* during roasting. The *fond* will become the basis in the *jus* or the pan gravy.

Preparation for *jus* or gravy
1. Place the pan on top of the stove and cook at a low temperature to evaporate the moisture. Do not stir. This is called clarifying the fat, which occurs at the point at which the water has evaporated and the *mirepoix* begins to fry. The *fond* will form on the bottom of the pan.
2. Now, pour off the excess fat.
3. The *fond* is then deglazed with stock, and then simmered.
4. Strain and skim off surface fat.
5. Season to taste.
   For *jus lie*:
6. Add enough diluted arrowroot to lightly thicken the sauce.
7. If arrowroot is unavailable, cornstarch may be used, but it will make the *jus lie* somewhat cloudy and will give it a less desirable texture.

Preparation for pan gravy
1. Caramelize *fond* and then pour off most of the fat, leaving only enough to help form an adequate amount of *roux* to thicken the gravy.
2. Add flour to the roasting pan, stir well, and cook for a few minutes.
3. Then add stock slowly to work out any lumps and to loosen *fond* from the bottom of the pan.
4. Simmer until gravy is well flavored and properly thickened.
5. Season to taste.
6. Strain.

Review the roasting procedure for meat:
1. Trim excess fat.
2. Lard/bard large cuts of meat if necessary.
3. Truss the item to improve shape.
4. Season.
5. Select an appropriate size pan and place item fat side up in pan.
6. Sear smaller items to assist in the caramelization before placing in the oven.
7. Preheat the oven—the temperature is determined by the type of meat, size, and weight.
8. Basting is suggested by using melted fats extruded from the item.
9. *Mirepoix* is added from one-half to three-quarters of an hour before the roast is done—approximately one ounce of *mirepoix* is used for each pound of meat.
10. Check for doneness by using a skewer, thermometer, or finger pressure.
11. Remove the roast five to fifteen degrees before it reaches desired temperature to allow for carryover cooking.
12. Allow for a resting period of about twenty to thirty minutes for juices to redistribute into the roast.
13. To minimize loss of juices, slice roast at service time.

Review the roasting procedure for poultry:
1. Tie or truss the poultry.
2. For nonfatty fowl, brush with oil or butter.
3. Sear, when applicable.
4. Choose an appropriate pan.
5. Place into a preheated oven.
6. Basting is required for most poultry by using the melted fats extruded from the food item.
7. *Mirepoix* is added during the roasting process.
8. Test for doneness by checking the color of the juices, using the finger pressure method, or twisting the leg joint.
9. No resting is required for small game or poultry.

REVIEW QUESTIONS

1. What type of cooking method is roasting?

2. What should meat be placed fat side up?

3. Why should a smaller cut be seared before the roasting process?

4. Why is *mirepoix* used during the roasting process?

5. When should the *mirepoix* be added?

6. What is carryover cooking?

7. What is trussing?

8. At what time should the roast be removed from the oven?

9. Why should the roast have a resting period before service?

10. At what temperature should the roast be held?

11. What two methods can be used to check for doneness in poultry that are not used with beef?

12. When making *jus lie*, why is arrowroot preferred over cornstarch?

13. When cooking poultry, what are the drippings comprised of that are left in the pan?

14. What is the basis of the *jus* or pan gravy?

15. What should basting be done with?

16. For nonfatty fowl, what should the poultry be brushed with to help with caramelization?

FOOD IS A WEAPON

DON'T WASTE IT !

BUY WISELY – COOK CAREFULLY – EAT IT ALL

FOLLOW THE NATIONAL WARTIME NUTRITION PROGRAM

"There are thieves not punished for stealing the most precious one: your time."

Napoleon Bonaparte

10

COST CONTROL

In most kitchens I have worked in during my career, controlling cost was one major effort the culinary team and leadership were engaged in. Controlling general expenses, labor, and COGS, or cost of goods, in particular, determine the success of your operation, financially speaking. You can have a kick-butt-exciting concept with quality food, innovative presentation, outgoing service, and entertaining ambiance, but if you cannot make more than you spend on it, the enterprise will be short lived; no matter how many industry and public accolades your chef and service may amass. This chapter is the basic primer for food cost management for the entry-level professional.

Beef up your bottom line from 4 percent to 14 percent by guarding against the following:

Purchasing
1. Purchasing too much
2. Purchasing for too high a cost
3. Not having detailed specifications- quality, weight, type
4. Not having a competitive purchasing policy
5. Not doing cost budget purchasing
6. Not controlling invoices and payments

Receiving
7. Dishonesty
8. No system of credits for low-quality or damaged goods, or goods not received
9. Lack of storage and/or no scales
10. Perishables left out of proper storage

Storage
11. Foods improperly placed in storage (e.g., fats, eggs, milk, near strong cheeses, fish, etc.)
12. Storage at wrong temperature
13. No daily inspection of stored goods
14. Poor sanitation in dry and refrigerated storage areas
15. Prices not marked in storeroom
16. No physical or perpetual inventory policy
17. Lack of single responsibility for food storage and issues

Issuing
18. No control or record of foods issued from storeroom
19. Permitting forced or automatic issues

Preparation

20. Excessive trim of vegetables and meats
21. No check on raw yield
22. No use of raw products for production of low-cost meals

Production

23. Overproduction
24. Wrong methods of cooking
25. Cooking at wrong temperatures
26. Cooking too long
27. No scheduling of foods to be processed (too early, too late)
28. Not using standard recipes
29. Not cooking in small batches

Service

30. No standard portion sizes
31. No standard size utensils for serving
32. No care of leftovers
33. No record of food produced and leaving production area
34. Carelessness (spillage, waste, cold food)

Sales

35. Food taken out of the establishment
36. Unrecorded sales and incorrect pricing: not charged or cash not turned in
37. No food popularity index or comparison of sales and inventory consumption
38. No sales analysis to direct trends
39. Poor menu pricing practices
40. Employee meal costs—overproduction of unauthorized meals

With a sound understanding and control of these forty points, managing your kitchen and controlling your cost of goods is actually quite simple, providing all culinary team members have the understanding and are engaged in the mission.

Common Weights and Measures:

Volume measurements

3 teaspoons	= 1 tablespoon
2 tablespoons	= 1 ounce
8 ounces	= 1 cup
2 cups	= 1 pint
2 pints	= 1 quart
4 quarts	= 1 gallon
128 ounces	= 1 gallon

Weight measurements

16 ounces	= 1 pound
1 gallon of water	= 8 pounds

Dipper or scoops (number indicates the scoopfuls in one quart)

6 equals ⅔ cup
8 equals ½ cup
10 equals ⅜ cup
12 equals ⅓ cup
16 equals ¼ cup

Hotel Pan Volumes

2-inch one-third pan	= 2½ quarts
4-inch one-third pan	= 4 quarts
2-inch half pan	= 4 quarts
4-inch half pan	= 6½ quarts
2-inch full pan	= 8 quarts
4-inch full pan	= 14 quarts

Low-Temperature Cooking

Originally invented in the late 1950s by Alto-Shaam, the Cook and Hold oven introduced low-temperature cooking to the food service industry and has remained the standard in cook-and-hold ovens. Often called "the Shaam," Alto-Shaam Cook and Hold ovens utilize exclusive Halo Heat technology, which surrounds the oven cavity with soft, gentle heat. This sealed heating environment traps meat's natural moisture, dramatically reducing meat shrinkage and promoting enzyme action and natural aging, providing naturally tender meat. This simplified cooking technology uses very little electricity, and since no hood ventilation is required, your operating costs will be very low.

Two major factors controlling shrinkage or cooking losses:
1. Temperature at which meat is cooked (higher temperature = more shrinkage)
2. Internal temperature of the meat (higher temperature = more shrinkage)

Four major factors involved in determining cooking times for meat:
1. Age of the meat—older meat cooks faster, shrinks more
2. Internal temperature prior to cooking—fire product (38°-40°F) in preheated oven; frozen meat has more shrinkage and cooks longer, resulting in lower quality
3. Desired degree of doneness—the higher the temperature, the longer the cooking time.
4. Quality and quantity of the protein

Example: Prime Rib	Raw	Cooked	Shrinkage	Yield
	Weight	Weight		
Conventional Cooking	17.90	12.90	5.00	72.1%
Slow Cooking	17.90	16.40	1.50	91.6%
Variance			3.50	
Cost Savings Potential				
1 rib @ $5.35			$18.73	
15 Ribs Per Week			$280.95	
Potential ROI Per Year			$14,609.40	

Food **Waste Issue**

Getting food from the farm to our fork eats up 10 percent of the total US energy budget, uses 50 percent of US land, and swallows 80 percent of all freshwater consumed in the United States. Yet, 40 percent of food in the United States today goes uneaten. Uneaten food ends up rotting in landfills as the single largest component of US municipal solid waste, where it accounts for almost 25 percent of US methane emissions. Reducing food losses by just 15 percent would be enough food to feed more than twenty-five million Americans every year.

The economic impact of this food waste:

- The value of food loss in the United States in 2008 was $165.6 billion.
- Forty-one percent of the value is losses in meat, poultry and fish
- Seven percent of the value is in vegetables, and 14 percent is in dairy products.
- Per capita, the value of food waste is estimated to be $390 a year, almost 10 percent of average food expenditures.
- For an average household of 2.4 people, this represents 654 pounds of food not eaten, at a retail value of $2.56 a day.

These numbers offer a compelling case for consumers to reduce their personal food waste.

Production costs of food waste:

The cost to landfill food waste in the United States reached $1.3 billion in 2008.
Production of the wasted food took three hundred million barrels of oil.

Losses in Food Service

According to the USDA, households and food service operations together lost eighty-six billion pounds of food in 2008, or 19 percent of the total US retail-level food supply.

Four to 10 percent of food purchased by restaurants becomes kitchen loss, both edible and inedible.

Another significant portion is served but never eaten, including large portions.

Staff behavior and kitchen culture can contribute to food waste.

Plate waste is a significant contributor to losses in food service, resulting primarily from large portions and undesired accompaniments.

On average, diners leave 17 percent of meals uneaten.

Fifty-five percent of these potential leftovers are not taken home.

Portion sizes have increased significantly over the past thirty years.

From 1982 to 2002, the average pizza slice grew 70 percent in calories.

The average chicken Caesar salad doubled in calories.

The average chocolate chip cookie quadrupled.

Today, portion sizes can be two to eight times larger than USDA or FDA standard serving sizes.

For this reason, I believe that looking for market-based approaches that promote reducing food waste while reducing the cost of production will be the most successful approach to combat the environmental, economic, and societal implications of food waste.

Here is an Example How to Write and Format a Recipe
Cranberry Cake with Pecans and Oats
Yield: 6 servings

Ingredients:
¼ cup oatmeal
¼ cup pecans, chopped
1 cup all-purpose flour
1¾ teaspoons baking powder
1 teaspoon salt
½ cup sugar
1 large egg
½ cup whole milk
1 stick (½ cup) unsalted butter, melted and cooled slightly
Grated zest from 1 orange
1 teaspoon vanilla
2 cups dried cranberries

Preparation:
1. Put oven rack in middle position and preheat oven to 375°F.
2. Spread oatmeal and pecans on bottom of 9-inch-square nonstick baking pan.
3. Whisk together flour, baking powder, salt, and sugar in medium bowl.
4. Whisk together egg, milk, butter, orange zest, and vanilla in large bowl.
5. Add flour mixture, whisking until just combined.
6. Spoon batter into baking pan, spreading evenly, then pour cranberries evenly over batter (berries will sink).
7. Bake until a knife inserted into center of cake comes out clean, approximately 25–30 minutes.
8. Cool in pan on a rack for 5 minutes.

Everyone Should Read a New Recipe Three Times
1. When someone gives you a new recipe, don't just start preparing it.
2. If possible, make a copy of the recipe so you can write on it. Check with your chef first: Some places are against copying recipes.
3. Read the recipe the first time from top to bottom to get a feel for the recipe. Picture in your mind how the dish will look when it is plated.
4. Read it again, slowly. Do you know how to do everything in the recipe? If not, ask.
5. Speaking of ingredients, do you have everything you need? If you are not 100% sure, then don't start anything until you check. If in doubt, ask your chef. In this second reading, determine if there are any traps in the recipe. For example: Marinate for four hours, soak the beans overnight, preheat the oven to 425°F, etc.
6. Now, read the recipe a third time to be sure that you have everything under control. Then, and only then, do you go to your work area and start getting all of your equipment and ingredients together.

Dark Chocolate Biscotti

Yield: 30 biscotti

Ingredients:
2 cups whole-wheat flour
2 tablespoons flaxseed
½ teaspoon baking soda
¼ teaspoon salt
⅓ cup granulated sugar
⅓ cup packed dark brown sugar
2 large egg whites
1 large egg
1 ½ teaspoons vanilla extract
⅔ cup dark chocolate chips (such as Hershey's)
¾ cup unsalted almonds

Preparation:
1. Preheat oven to 350°F.
2. Weigh or lightly spoon flour into dry measuring cups; level with a knife.
3. Combine flour, flaxseed, soda, and salt in a bowl, stirring with a whisk.
4. Combine sugars, egg whites, and egg in a bowl; beat with a mixer at high speed for 2 minutes.
5. Add vanilla; mix well. Add flour mixture to egg mixture; stir until combined.
6. Fold in chocolate and almonds. Divide dough into 3 equal portions.
7. Roll each portion into a 6-inch-long roll. Arrange rolls 3 inches apart on a baking sheet lined with parchment paper. Pat to a 1-inch thickness.
8. Bake at 350°F for 28 minutes or until firm.
9. Remove rolls from baking sheet; cool 10 minutes on a wire rack.
10. Cut rolls diagonally into 30 (½-inch) slices. Place, cut sides down, on baking sheet.
11. Reduce oven temperature to 325°F; bake 7 minutes.
12. Turn cookies over; bake 7 minutes (cookies will be slightly soft in center but will harden as they cool).
13. Remove from baking sheet; cool on wire rack.

DID YOU KNOW?

Biscotti, more correctly known as *biscotti di Prato*, also known as *cantuccini*, are twice-baked biscuits originating in the city of Prato. Pastry chef Antonio Mattei introduced his variation, what is now accepted as the traditional recipe for biscotti, at the second World's Fair in Paris in 1867.

Since they are very dry, biscotti traditionally are served with a drink, into which they may be dunked. In Italy they are typically served as an after-dinner dessert with a Tuscan fortified wine called *vin santo*.

REVIEW QUESTIONS

1. How many ounces are in a #10 can?

2. What does the number on the scoop/dipper indicate?

3. What is the capacity of a 2½-inch hotel pan?

4. How many #8 scoops does a hotel pan yield?

5. One tablespoon yields how many teaspoons?

6. How many eight-ounce cans are in one case?

7. What can you do with overripe bananas?

8. How can you utilize old bread and rolls?

9. Traditionally, what is the most expensive breakfast item?

10. Name the three expense groups and include examples.

11. Name two major factors controlling shrinkage or cooking losses.

12. Name four major factors involved in determining cooking times for meat.

"An invasion of armies can be resisted, but not an idea whose time has come."

Victor Hugo

11

SUSTAINABILITY

Definition
Sustainability, in a broad sense, is the capacity to endure or biological systems remaining productive over time. Sustainability also means long-term maintenance of well-being of the natural world and the responsible use of all natural resources. The sustainability movement focuses on organic foods, foods produced without synthetic pesticides, artificial fertilizers, hormones, antibiotics, or genetic modification.

Global Issues
One billion people worldwide do not have secure access to food, including thirty-six million in the United States. National and international food and agricultural policies have helped to create the global food crisis but can also help to fix the system.

Health Issues
- Seventy-six million Americans are sickened, 325,000 are hospitalized, and 5,000 die each year because of food-borne illnesses, according to the Centers for Disease Control.
- **RBGH (recombinant bovine growth hormone)** is a genetically engineered hormone injected into dairy cows to make them produce more milk. Many countries have banned the use of RBGH, including Canada and the European Union, but not the United States, where it is used extensively.
- Pesticide concentrations in dust collected from farm workers' homes were five times higher than those in nonfarm workers' homes.
- The USDA estimates that between 1970 and 2000, the average daily calorie intake in the US increased by 24.5 percent, or about 530 calories.
- Six hormones are implanted in beef cattle for no other reason than to make the cows grow faster so they can be sold sooner.
- Ninety percent of all US feedlot cattle are hormone implanted.
- Human deaths related to poor diet and physical inactivity is second only to tobacco as the leading preventable cause of death in the United States.
- One-third of children and adolescents are overweight or obese. High-calorie, sugar-laden processed foods, coupled with our sedentary lifestyles, are growing our waistlines and contributing to serious health issues like diabetes, heart ailments, and cancers. Kids should be served healthy meals, not soda and junk food.

Factory Farming
Virtually all the meat, eggs, and dairy products that you find in the supermarket come from animals raised in confinement in large facilities called CAFOs, or "Confined Animal Feeding Operations." These highly mechanized operations provide a year-round supply of food at a reasonable price. Although the food is cheap and convenient, there is growing recognition that factory farming creates a host of problems, including animal stress and abuse, pollution, and unnecessary use of hormones, antibiotics, and other drugs, as well as the loss of small family farms and, last but not least, food with less nutritional value.

Unnatural Diets

Animals raised in factory farms are given diets designed to boost their productivity and lower costs. The main ingredients are genetically modified grain and soy that are kept at artificially low prices by government subsidies. To further cut costs, the feed may also contain "by-product feedstuff" such as municipal garbage, stale pastry, chicken feathers, and candy. Until 1997, US cattle were also being fed meat that had been trimmed from other cattle, in effect turning herbivores into carnivores. This unnatural practice is believed to be the underlying cause of BSE, or "mad cow disease."

Caged Animals

Most of the nation's chickens, turkeys, and pigs are also being raised in confinement; they suffer an even worse fate than the grazing animals. Tightly packed into cages, sheds, or pens, they cannot practice their normal behaviors, such as rooting, grazing, and roosting. Laying hens are crowded into cages that are so small that there is not enough room for all of the birds to sit down at one time. They cannot escape the stench of their own manure. Meat and eggs from these animals are lower in a number of key vitamins and omega-3 fatty acids.

Environmental Issues

- Fifteen hundred miles—the distance the average food product travels to get to your grocery store.
- Thirty thousand eight hundred tons—the amount of greenhouse gas emissions every year transporting food.
- Six percent of US farms generate 75 percent of all commercial agricultural production.
- In 2007, 63 percent of hens sold for egg production and 67 percent of chickens sold for meat production were raised on farms that managed more than 100,000 birds.
- In 2007, 87 percent of all hogs sold in the United States were raised on farms that managed more than 5,000 hogs.
- Agriculture subsidies in 2007 totaled $8 billion.
- Ten percent of eligible farms received 60 percent of all farm subsidies the same year.
- When animals are raised in feedlots or cages, they deposit large amounts of manure in a small amount of space. To cut costs, it is dumped as close to the feedlot as possible. As a result, the surrounding soil is overloaded with nutrients, which can cause ground and water pollution. When animals are raised outdoors on pasture, their manure is spread over a wide area of land, making it a welcome source of organic fertilizer, not a "waste management problem."
- The annual cost of environmental damage caused by US industrial farming is $34.7 billion.
- Three thousand acres of productive farmland are lost to development each day in the United States.
- Millions of gallons of untreated manure are held in open-air pits and pollute the surrounding air, land, and water.
- Thirty-five thousand miles of rivers in twenty-two states and groundwater in at least seventeen states have been polluted by cattle waste.

Pesticides

Cancers, autism, and neurological disorders are associated with the use of pesticides, especially amongst farm workers and their communities. What pesticides are in your food, and what are their effects?

Back to Pasture

Since the late 1990s, a growing number of ranchers have stopped sending their animals to the feedlots to be fattened on grain, soy, and other supplements. Instead, they are keeping their animals' home on the range, where they forage on pasture, their native diet. These new-age ranchers do not treat their livestock with hormones or feed them growth-promoting additives. As a result, the animals grow at a natural pace. For these reasons and more, grass-fed animals live low-stress lives and are so healthy there is no reason to treat them with antibiotics or other drugs.

Grass Farming

Raising animals on pasture requires more knowledge and skill than sending them to a feedlot. For example, in order for grass-fed beef to be succulent and tender, the cattle need to forage on high-quality grasses and legumes, especially in the months prior to slaughter. This nutritious and natural diet requires healthy soil and careful pasture management so that the plants are maintained at an optimal stage of growth. Because high-quality pasture is the key to high-quality animal products, many pasture-based ranchers refer to themselves as "grass farmers" rather than "ranchers." They raise great grass; the animals do all the rest.

More Nutritious

A major benefit of raising animals on pasture is that their products are healthier for you. Compared with feedlot meat, meat from grass-fed beef, bison, lamb, and goats has less total fat, saturated fat, cholesterol, and calories. It also has more vitamin E, beta-carotene, vitamin C, and a number of health-promoting fats, including omega-3 fatty acids and "conjugated linoleic acid," or CLA.

When you choose to eat meat, eggs, and dairy products from animals raised on pasture, you are improving the welfare of the animals, helping to put an end to environmental degradation, helping small-scale ranchers and farmers make a living from the land, helping to sustain rural communities, and giving your family the healthiest possible food. It's a win-win-win-win situation.

The issues are many and the stakes are high. There is no single solution for this complex issue, and no quick fix, either, for a system with its root cause going back to the policies of the seventies. The public not only deserves better—a food chain with transparency and no doubts about its integrity—we owe it to our children to leave them a better place.

"We, as chefs and professionals, can contribute greatly.
I feel we have an obligation to not only educate our employees,
But our guests as well, tackling the issues at stake,
Getting involved, and being part of the solution.
Educate your family, friends, neighbors, schools, and community."
Peter Gebauer

DID YOU KNOW?

Growing Power **will build the first five-story vertical farm in the country**
The farm will have south-facing greenhouse areas for the year-round
production of plants, vegetables, and herbs. The building will provide
educational classrooms, conference spaces, a demonstration kitchen,
food processing and storage areas, freezers, and loading docks to further support our mission as a local and national resource for learning
about urban, sustainable food production.
**The vertical farm will be a hub of economic activity, community
building, educational opportunities, and resource sharing for the
Milwaukee community and the world.**

How Sustainable is Our Seafood?

Our food chain faces more challenges caused by a number of issues, not only land based, but in the oceans, rivers and lakes as well.

On average, the human body is 60 percent water. The earth is 70 percent water. Only 1 percent of that water is accessible freshwater. And, most of that, about 70 percent, is used for agriculture (irrigation) and for raising livestock. One very beautiful thing about aquaculture: you won't ever see fish standing in line at the water fountain waiting to take a drink. According to the National Geographic Society Water Initiative, it takes:

- 1,799 gallons of water to produce one pound of beef.
- 576 gallons of water to produce one pound of pork.
- 468 gallons of water to produce one pound of chicken.

How many gallons of water do you think it takes to produce one simple little chicken egg?

Aquaculture: With a growing world population and marine fisheries in decline, fisheries experts have long hoped that aquaculture might one day take up the slack. In some ways it already is, but a growing number of marine scientists believe that parts of the industry may instead contribute to the further decline of marine resources. The intense controversy pertains to which species are being farmed and how they are being farmed. Salmon, shrimp, and tuna are examples of carnivorous animals that must be fed other fish. Most farms raising these species ultimately consume more fish than they produce. The profit motive also inclines many farms to implement large-scale industrial practices that can result in pollution, the destruction of marine habitat, and a tendency to generate diseases that pose a risk to both wild fish and consumers. And there are a number of other contributing issues:

Overfishing

- Catching fish faster than they can reproduce is the single biggest threat to ocean ecosystems.
- Seventy-five percent of the world's fisheries are either fully exploited or have collapsed.
- The global fishing fleet is operating at two times the sustainable level—too many boats chasing a dwindling number of fish.
- Management agencies need to set realistic catch limits that help ensure the health of species and preserve their roles in the ecosystem. Alaska wild salmon are one example of a fishery that is thriving under sensible limits and careful management.

Illegal Fishing

- The fewer fish there are, the more desperate we become to catch them, and this leads to illegal fishing.
- At least a quarter of the world's catch is illegal. One example is the wasteful practice of shark finning, where the sharks' fins are removed and the rest of the animal is thrown overboard to die a slow death. This practice, while illegal in over one hundred nations, continues to threaten shark populations worldwide.

Management Plans

- About one-fifth of total global fisheries production is poached.
- The biggest issue is pirate fishermen taking fish outside the scope of an existing management plan. These violations include taking undersize fish, fishing in closed areas during seasonal closures, using illegal gear, or taking more fish than is allocated. Slow-growing fish that breed late in life are naturally vulnerable to over fishing. Patagonian tooth fish, a.k.a. Chilean sea bass, have been particularly affected by pirate fishing. Poaching is rampant, especially in remote waters where law enforcement is difficult.
- As long-established fish populations have collapsed, fishing has moved and intensified in Africa and the Pacific. Pirates that ignore regulations and steal fish are denying the poorest regions of the world much-needed food, security, and income. While poor nations are implicated in illegal fishing, developed nations are most to blame.

Habitat Damage

- Oceans never get a rest. Many fishing practices destroy fish and the places they live. Among different fishing gear, bottom trawling and dredging are top offenders. Trawls and dredges that drag across the seafloor can destroy the delicate ecosystems that provide shelter, food, and breeding grounds for fish and other species. In heavily trawled areas, it's the equivalent of clear cutting a forest several times a year. In Alaskan waters alone, over one million pounds of deepwater corals and sponges are destroyed each year. Marine life and seafloor communities have no chance to recover—parts of the North Sea off Denmark are trawled up to four hundred times a year!
- In 2003, California replaced spot prawn trawls with traps, reducing seafloor damage and helping the state's rock-fish population recover.
- In general, traps and pots cause less seafloor damage and catch fewer unintended species than other types of fishing gear.

By catch

- Two hundred thousand loggerheads and fifty thousand leatherback turtles are caught annually.
- Hundreds of thousands of seabirds are killed annually when they become entangled in driftnets or caught on long-line hooks when they dive for bait.
- Worldwide, one out of every four fish caught is discarded dead or dying as "by catch." One of the biggest offenders is the shrimp fishery.
- For every pound of shrimp caught, the shrimp industry discards almost twice that in other species. It can be ten times this in some areas. By catch doesn't just include fish—turtles, seabirds, and other animals also suffer.
- By catch is often caused by less selective fishing gear like long lines or bottom trawls. Long lines have baited hooks and can extend for fifty miles or more. When cast out and left to "soak," long lines attract anything that swims by, from sharks to sea turtles. Bottom trawls drag nets across the seafloor, catching everything in their paths.
- Fishermen truly don't want to haul in by catch—it wastes their time and wears out their gear. Boats need to be outfitted with more selective gear to reduce this waste and to help preserve our oceans.
- In contrast, gear like hook-and-line fishing limits by catch because fishermen can quickly release unwanted catch from their hooks since lines are reeled in soon after a fish takes the bait.

Benefits of Better Fishing Gear

In places where management agencies have enforced the use of better fishing gear, by catch and habitat damage have been reduced. This includes requiring devices that allow turtles to escape from nets, the use of less harmful "circle hooks," and a movement away from harmful methods such as bottom trawls and dredge.

Innovative Management is Essential

Creating "Marine Protected Areas": Similar to state and national parks on land, Marine Protected Areas preserve under-sea habitat, allowing marine wildlife to recover and thrive. These safe havens result in larger, more abundant fish, plants. and other marine life.

Sustainable Aquaculture: In order to be truly sustainable, aquaculture operations need to operate in ways that do not harm marine ecosystems or coastal communities, and that neither consume more resources than they produce nor rob future generations of a healthy ocean. In China, millions of people depend on farms that raise carp, an herbivorous fish that requires no fishmeal. Carp are omnivorous species like catfish and tilapia that can be farmed with very little need of fishmeal or fish oil. Farms that raise shellfish like abalone, clams, oysters, and mussels also produce a net gain in protein for a hungry world. These kinds of aquaculture are best suited for truly taking pressure off our overexploited oceans.

The Monterey Bay Aquarium has identified seafood that is "Super Green," meaning that it is good for human health and does not harm the oceans. This list highlights products that are currently on the Seafood Watch "Best Choices" (green) list, are low in environmental contaminants, and are good sources of long-chain omega-3 fatty acids. The Super Green list includes seafood that meets the following criteria: low levels of contaminants such as mercury and PCBs, and the daily minimum of omega-3s.

Aquaculture is important and valuable. It is one of the best ways to produce the protein we need to feed an ever-growing human population. But, it must be sound aquaculture. We'll never achieve ecologically sustainable aquaculture without demanding ecologically sustainable agriculture, too. They are intertwined.

Oh, that one single chicken egg—it takes 55 gallons of water to produce.

Again, we as chefs and professionals can contribute greatly, and I feel a compelling obligation to not only educate our employees, but our guests as well, to take action and be part of the solution. Incorporate more sustainable seafood in your menus. Request your suppliers to support you in sourcing and obtaining sustainable wild and farmed species. Educate yourself, your team, and guests to make a lasting difference.

Mission

Our objective is to identify, present, and debate current issues and information on farming issues, sustainability, product authentication, global trends, biomass, annual catch limits, aquaculture production methods and sources, and how the conditions of each should impact our decision processes. This information will be periodically derived from leading experts in academia, research, fishery organizations, and other credible contributing sources, allowing our management team to make the most informed seafood purchasing decisions. We will establish an ongoing auditing and sampling program that helps ensure that we are providing the great quality and value seafood that our customers expect.

Vision

We are dedicated to responsible fishing practices and the healthy stewardship of the world's marine resources. Our procurement process will relay on guidance and recommendations of the Seafood Watch program as well as the Marine Stewardship Council and issued government regulations. We will consult with distinguished conservation groups, such as Ocean Trust, to help us employ best practices. In addition, we will reach out to our suppliers and the fishermen, from whom we source product around the globe, to promote environmentally sound fishing and aquaculture.

We are proud to embark on this venture and will focus our energy and efforts on educating and engaging our team members and customers in support of constructive projects that help advance the sustainability of food resources, both land based and marine, and recognize its critical link to coastal communities that depend on the sea.

The oceans are resilient, and fish populations can rebound—if we give them a chance.

Through our actions, we intend to be part of the solution.

> *"What makes the desert beautiful is that somewhere it hides a well."*

Antoine de Saint-Exupery

Smoked Asian Fish Cakes
Yield: 24-26 one ounce cakes

Ingredients:
½ cup mayonnaise
1 teaspoon Dijon mustard
1 egg
½ cup onion, fine brunoise
½ cup red yellow pepper, fine brunoise
1 teaspoon extra virgin olive oil
¼ bunch chives, sliced
Salt and pepper to taste
½ teaspoon Cajun seasoning
1 pound smoked boneless silver fin
1 cup panko bread crumbs

Procedure:
1. Combine mayonnaise, mustard, and egg, and chill.
2. Sauté onion and pepper in extra virgin olive oil until softened. Cool down.
3. Combine onion, red pepper, mayonnaise, mustard, egg, parsley, salt, pepper, and Cajun seasoning.
4. Gently fold the mayonnaise mixture into fish and panko bread crumbs; careful to not shred the flesh of the meat.
5. Adjust seasoning to taste.
6. Shape and chill for one hour.
7. Pan fry and serve with tartar sauce or aioli.

DID YOU KNOW?

Asian carp is a "green fish," environmentally friendly because it eats so low on the food chain. It's high in heart-healthy omega-3 fatty acids and is inexpensive. Asian carp are low in mercury because they don't eat other fish. They also grow so quickly, there's little time to accumulate it.

Asian carp are not native to the U.S., and there are three types that cause fishermen the most concern: the bighead, the silver carp, and the black carp. The fish can multiply quickly and threaten the food that bass, paddlefish, and other species depend on.

Efforts to keep them out of the Great Lakes include spending millions of dollars on electrical barriers. In the Illinois River, the invasive fish erupt around motorboats like popcorn in a hot pan. The fish are swimming in growing numbers deeper into Tennessee through locks and dams on the Cumberland and Tennessee rivers. A commercial catfish fisherman in Tennessee has hauled in as much as 5,000 pounds of silver carp in a day from the northern portion of Kentucky Lake.

Silver carp were brought to the U.S. from China, mainly to clean up the algae and detritus in catfish ponds and sewage lagoons. But massive flooding on the Mississippi River since the early 1990s sent water across ponds, allowing the carp to escape into the major waterways.

REVIEW QUESTIONS

1. What does CAFO stand for?

2. Define genetic engineering (GE).

3. What is a GMO?

4. What is high fructose corn syrup?

5. What does rBGH stand for?

6. Define sustainable.

7. Explain TBQH.

8. Define organic.

9. What are wet mills?

10. What is fish meal?

11. What is long lining?

12. What is omega-3?

13. Explain the term once frozen.

14. What are the snow crab species we use called, and how many are there?

15. Name the tuna species you know.

"Give a fish to a man; he has food for a day. Teach a man to fish; he learns a skill for life."

Fan Li

12

SUSHI

Irasshaimase! (Welcome!)
According to the Japanese, sushi made its debut approximately thirteen hundred years ago. At that time sushi was far from what it is now. The preparation of sushi was done as a technique to preserve fish through the use of salt. During the Edo period (about six hundred years ago), the first culinary preparation of sushi as we know it today (fish and rice) was carried out in Tokyo.
Today, sushi is divided into two main culinary forms: Tokyo and Osaka style.
In Tokyo, sliced fish is put on a bed of rice. In Osaka, sushi is prepared by slicing fish, laying it on rice and then pressing it in a wooden box or rolling it with seaweed and rice.
Legend has it that sushi is the original "finger food" enjoyed by Japanese card players hundreds of years ago. It is said that seaweed paper was rolled on the outside of sushi to avoid "sticky fingers" while playing!

Types of Sushi
Although there are many different ways to prepare sushi, we will learn how to prepare the most popular varieties. These are:

Nigiri–Zushi
Rectangular bars of vinegared rice topped with a dab of wasabi (Japanese horseradish) and a thin slice of
Fresh raw fish.

Inari–Zushi
Soybean pouch filled with rice, and vegetable of seafood.

Maki–Zushi
A sheet of seaweed paper is coated with vinegared rice. Fresh raw fish and/or vegetables are placed in the center, and then it is rolled and sliced.

Sushi Accompaniment
Everyone who comes to eat at the sushi bar knows that there are so-called condiments to be enjoyed with the sushi. You may not realize that each one has a specific purpose other than that of just a simple flavoring.

Gari	This is thinly sliced pickled ginger. It should be eaten a little at a time between different varieties of sushi to freshen the palate.
Wasabi	This is green Japanese horseradish. It is made from a green knobby root that is ground. It is a very powerful seasoning that makes the fishy taste of sushi disappear by momentarily paralyzing the mouth.
Shoyu	This salty dipping sauce has historical significance in that its taste reminds us of what sushi tasted like when the preparation was merely used as an act of conservation.
Ocha (agari)	This is Japanese green tea. It is very refreshing as it rinses the mouth and tongue of fat buildup from the fish. For this reason, plenty of tea is served in a large mug.

Sushi Etiquette

Sushi was originally a finger food, and while chopsticks are often used, they are by no means mandatory or as easy to manage as fingers!

To eat sushi, pick it up at one end, turn it upside down and lightly dip it in the soy sauce. It should always be the fish that hits your taste buds first, not the rice. If using chopsticks, never stab the chopsticks into the center of a bowl of rice, as this is bad luck! Do not stab the sushi or pick it up vertically—the sushi will most likely break in half—but rather horizontally, like a forklift, from the side.

Fondness for soy sauce leads some people to soak the rice part of the sushi in it. This is not recommended, as it makes the rice fall apart and obliterates the taste of both rice and topping. Soy sauce should act as a compliment to the foods it is eaten with.

Sushi Rice

Next to the absolute freshness of the fish you use for sushi, the preparation of the rice is of utmost importance. There are three main types of rice available: medium grain Japanese rice, white long grain Chinese rice, and instant rice. The taste and texture of cooked rice depend on the type and quality of the rice, so you should take great care when selecting it. For sushi, we recommend white, medium grain Japanese rice. If you are not familiar with rice, go to a well-stocked Asian market and purchase a package of rice especially marked "for sushi." If it's not available, the next best thing is white, medium grain rice. If the package is see-through, look for grain that is uniform in size and slightly transparent.

Preparation

Rice increases in volume as it cooks, anywhere from two to two and a half times, depending on the type of rice you use. If you plan to cook a lot of rice, an automatic rice cooker will make your work much easier. For the price, it's a good investment. However, a Dutch oven or a pot with a fitted lid and good heat distribution will do just as well. As a general rule, equal amounts of rice and water are needed for sushi rice. But medium grain rice grown in California may need a little more water (maybe one-quarter cup).

For regular unseasoned cooked rice, one cup of rice with one and one-quarter cups of water will make moist, fluffy rice.

1. Measure rice carefully.
2. Wash rice in a big bowl of water. Rub grains gently; wet grains break easily. This is done to remove bran and polishing agents.
3. Drain off water and repeat steps two and three until water is almost clear.
4. Leave rice to sit for at least thirty minutes in summer and one hour in winter. This allows ample time for the rice to absorb water.
5. In the cooking pot, mix rice and the correct amount of water. Cover with a lid.
6. Place pot over medium heat until water boils. If the quantity of rice is large, cook rice over high heat from the beginning.
7. When it begins to boil, turn heat to high and cook for one minute. Never lift the lid while the rice is cooking. If the lid bounces from the pressure of the steam, it is best to place a weighted object on the lid.
8. Turn heat to low and cook for four to five minutes. Be careful not to let it boil over. At this point, the pot will begin to steam heavily; this is due to small pores in the rice that open and release steam.
9. Reduce heat to lowest setting for ten minutes. As rice absorbs water it becomes plump and is liable to burn. It is important that your stove be on its lowest setting.
10. Turn off the heat and let the rice stand, covered, for ten minutes. This allows the rice to settle while the cooking process completes itself.

Automatic Rice Cooker

The automatic rice cooker makes perfect rice. Put washed rice into the cooker and add water. There are measurement lines on the inside of the cooker for rice and water levels. Cover and turn on. The cooker adjusts temperatures and times automatically.

Preparing Vinegar Mixture

Sushi rice is sweet and sticky. This is achieved by combining rice with a mixture of vinegar, salt, and sugar. The table below shows appropriate quantities of rice, water, and elements for the vinegar mixture.

Prepared Rice	Rice Vinegar	Sugar	Salt
2½ cups	2 tablespoons	1 tablespoon	1 teaspoon
5 cups	3½ tablespoons	1 tablespoon	1½ teaspoons
7½ cups	5 tablespoons	1½ tablespoons	2 teaspoons
10 cups	7 tablespoons	2 tablespoons	3 teaspoons (1 tablespoon)

Tossing Rice with Vinegar Mixture

You will need a large nonmetallic tub (preferably glass or unpolished wood) and a large wooden spatula.

1. Wash mixing tub well and dry with a kitchen towel.
2. Put cooked rice into mixing tub and spread it evenly over the bottom.
3. Sprinkle vinegar mixture (see above) generously over rice. You may not need all the mixture. Do not create excess liquid in tub.
4. With a large wooden spatula, mix rice with a slicing motion.
5. While you mix, have a helper fan the tub, or use an electric fan. This is not to cool sushi rice but to remove excess moisture.
6. Keep sushi rice in tub, covered with a damp cloth.

Fish for Sushi

Fresh fish that is eaten raw as sashimi and sushi must be prepared with fish that has not been out of the water for more than twenty-four hours and has been properly chilled. Most fish has a shelf life of about five days.

When buying fish, a reputable fish shop can generally provide fish of better quality than that found packaged in a supermarket. When buying your fish for sushi or sashimi, ask the fishmonger to cut it for you.

If you are in doubt as to the freshness of a piece of fish, do not eat it raw. Cook it to your personal taste or marinate it and then broil. Also, no freshwater fish are eaten raw in sushi because of the possibility of parasite content.

Checking Fish for Freshness

The following are ways to check fish for freshness:

1. Mild characteristic odor, but not too strong and never "fishy."
2. Bright, full, clear eyes, not milky or sunken.
3. Bright, red gills, not muddy gray, and free of slime.
4. Bright sheen on scales.
5. Unblemished scales that adhere strongly to the skin; no reddish patches on ventral area.
6. Firm or rigid body when pressed with fingers.
7. Elastic, firm flesh that does not separate easily from the bones and doesn't indent when handled.
8. Freshly cut appearance with no "leathery" traces of yellowing.
9. No visible signs of "dryness."
10. Fresh fish tastes sweet and often has cucumber like odor.

Storing Fish

Since shellfish and fish are the most perishable foods, they should be used as quickly as possible. In the event that storage is required:

1. Wash the fish in cold, salty water. Make sure to wash the stomach cavity well. Remove excess water with paper towels, then wrap in waxed paper or freezer wrap. Place in the refrigerator and handle as little as possible.

2. Frozen fish should be kept frozen solid in freezer wrap or a suitable container. Do not thaw frozen fish at room temperature before cooking. Thawing frozen fish is best achieved at refrigerator temperature. Once the fish has been thawed, use it immediately. Never refreeze fish that has been thawed. It is recommended that you not keep frozen fish for more than three months.

3. To remove odor from utensils, wash with a solution of baking soda and water (about one teaspoon soda to one quart of water).

4. To get rid of "fishy" smells on the hands or cutting board, rub with lemon juice, sliced lemon, vinegar, or salt before washing, then rinse well. A small amount of toothpaste rubbed on the hands also acts as a good deodorizer.

Slicing Fish

It is important that you have a very sharp, very clean knife available for cutting the fish. Raw fish, while delicate, is also very difficult to cut unless the knife is literally razor sharp. You may want to get a knife specifically for this purpose. Also remember that any time you are butchering a raw product, it must be done in the most sterile of environments. Ensure that the cutting board you use is clean and in good shape (no deep gouges).

Nori or Seaweed

Nori is available in sheets which come in three different sizes. Three different types are available: seasoned, no seasoned, and toasted. When buying nori, make sure the package is well sealed and free of rips or holes.

To store:

1. Keep in a cool place, preferably the refrigerator or freezer. Open packages should be kept in an airtight container, or wrapped in foil, plastic, or freezer wrap to keep out the air. Well-sealed nori will keep indefinitely in the freezer.

2. Keep in a dark place. Light will affect the flavor of nori.

Avoid any moisture. If it loses its crispness, lightly toast it over a burner.

DID YOU KNOW?

The original type of sushi, known today as *nare-zushi*, was first developed in Southeast Asia and spread to south China before being introduced to Japan sometime around the eighth century. Fish was salted and wrapped in fermented rice for preservation. During the Edo period, "quick sushi," or *Haya-zushi*, emerged; now both rice and fish could be consumed at the same time, and the dish became unique to Japanese culture. It was the first time that rice was not being used for fermentation. Rice was now mixed with vinegar, with fish, vegetables, and dried foodstuff added.

REVIEW QUESTIONS

1. What two styles, in terms of culinary forms, is sushi divided into?

2. Why was seaweed paper rolled on the outside of sushi (still carried on today!)?

3. What is wasabi?

4. Why should you not use soy sauce when eating sushi?

5. What type of rice is recommended for use when making sushi?

6. When making sushi rice, what is the recommended ratio of rice to water?

7. When making sushi rice, what is the ratio of vinegar and sugar to salt?

8. How many types of nori are available?

9. What is the difference between a regular sushi roll and an "inside-out" (uramaki) roll?

10. What ingredients make up a California roll?

11. What is tobiko?

12. What is the difference between sushi and sashimi?

13. Why is pickled ginger served with sushi?

14. What is temaki?

15. Why do you wrap the sushi mat in plastic wrap?

16. Why is it important to have warm water in a bowl next to you when making sushi?

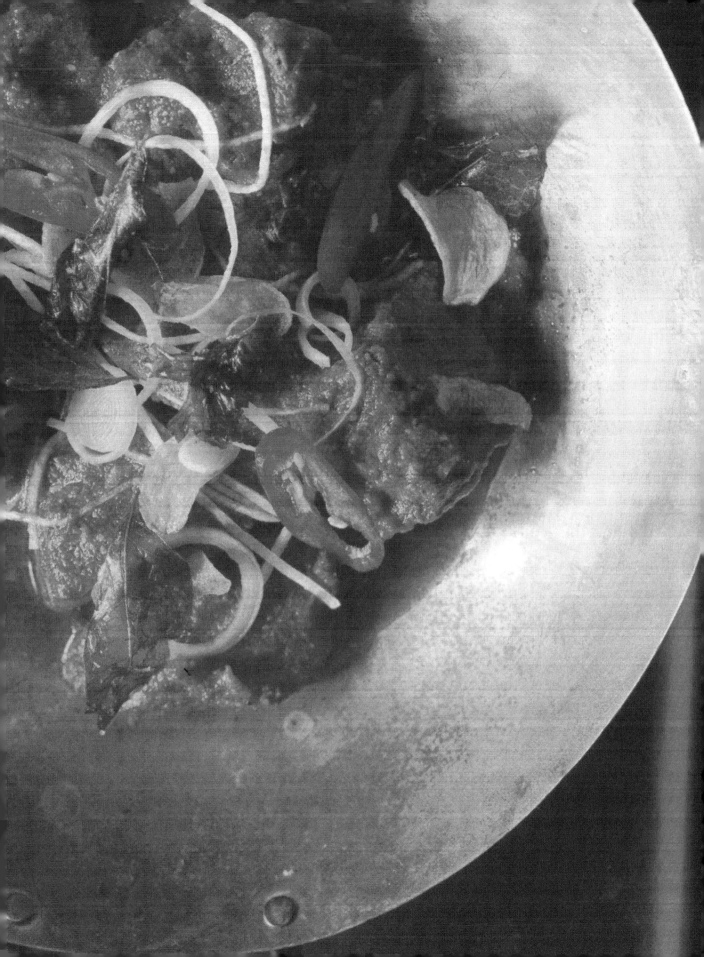

"A master can tell you what he expects of you. A teacher, though, awakens your own expectations."

Patricia Neal, Actress

13

WOK

Introduction

The earliest woks were not woks at all, but cast-iron pans with sloping sides great for tossing and stirring a lot of food easily. Developed as a result of the frugal use of fuel, historians also think that there is a connection between woks and the helmets and shields of the invading Mongols. A wide variety of different materials, sizes, and shapes is available nowadays. The traditional wok made from uncoated carbon steel is the most popular one. This material conducts heat well and is the most economical to purchase.

There are many words for the wok in different cultures and languages:

Cantonese Chinese:	woo
Mandarin Chinese:	*guo*, "cooking pot"
Indonesia:	*penggorengan* or *wajan*
Malaysia:	*kuali*, "small wok"
Philippines:	*wadjang*
Japan:	*chukanabe*
India:	*cheena chatty* ("Chinese pot")

Chinese Regional Cuisine

Chinese dishes may be categorized as one of the Eight Culinary Traditions of China, also called the "Eight Regional Cuisines" and the "Eight Cuisines of China."
The most popular culinary traditions are:

Yue (Cantonese): Guangdong (flavors should be well balanced, spices used in modest amounts, primary ingredients at the peak of their freshness and quality)
Chuan: Sichuan (bold flavors, particularly the pungency and spiciness from garlic and chili; the unique Sichuan pepper)
Lu: Shandong (Beijing; greatest contribution to Chinese cuisine is brewing vinegars)
Su Huaiyang (Jiangsu; tends to have a sweet/sour side to it and is almost never spicy)

Then there are these regions/traditions:

Hui: Anhui
Min: Fujian
Xiang: Hunan (Can include Xiangjiang Region, Dongting Lake and Xiangxi styles)
Zhe: Zhejiang (Can include Hangzhou, Ningbo, and Shaoxing styles)

Seasoning the Wok

Only iron and steel woks need to be seasoned. Stainless steel woks do not need this treatment, as they are far less porous than iron or steel woks. However with stainless steel woks, more oil is required to prevent the food from sticking and burning. Seasoning a steel wok enables foods to glide smoothly over the cooking surface of the wok. In a properly seasoned wok, one should be able to make perfect omelets. If the omelets even stick ever so slightly, then the wok is not properly seasoned and should be reseasoned.

There are two methods for seasoning the iron or steel wok.

1. To season a new or to reseason an old rusty wok, thoroughly scrub it inside and out with soap and a steel wool scouring pad to remove the manufacturer's protective coating on a new wok or the rust on an old one. Rinse thoroughly with hot water. Some manufacturers apply a coating that is hard to remove, so set the wok on the stove, fill it with water and boil it for several minutes until the coating dissolves. Pour out the water and scrub the surface clean with steel wool and soap.

    Set the clean wok over high heat. Heat until a few drops of water sprinkled into the wok immediately turn into dancing beads. While the pan is heating, it will change from shiny steel grey to blue, purple, red, and, finally, black. Dip several sheets of wadded-up paper towel into peanut or corn oil and wipe the oil on the entire inside surface of the wok (you may want to use long-handled tongs to hold the towels). Reduce heat to low and let the wok sit over the heat for fifteen minutes to absorb the oil—the color changes will continue and, hopefully, the bottom of the wok will darken. In time and with frequent use, the entire wok will turn black. If the surface looks dry, wipe with another thin film of oil. Remove wok from the burner and let it cool. Reheat the wok and repeat the oiling and heating process once more before using it for stir-frying.

2. Another more thorough method of seasoning a wok is to brush polyunsaturated cooking oil on the cooking surface of the wok and then place the wok into an oven at 300°F for four hours. The oil in the wok will become pooled while heating in the oven, so about every hour or so, take your brush and brush the oil up around the sides of the wok and continue heating. Obviously, woks that have plastic or wooden handles should not be put in the oven.

New woks may cause a slight metallic taste in the first two or three dishes that are cooked in it, but, after use, the metallic taste disappears.

A wok's worst enemies are soap and scouring pads—they'll remove any seasoning the wok has acquired.

After cooking foods in the wok, it is best to run very hot water into it and clean the surface of the wok with a bamboo brush or plastic scour. If you watch a Chinese cook in a large restaurant, you will see him (yes, I think men are the best cooks!) keep the wok on the stove, make it hot again and then dump some water into the wok and, as it is sizzling, scrub it quickly with a bamboo brush and then dump the water before starting to make a new order. The whole process takes maybe five seconds and the wok is clean.

After you have washed your wok, dry it thoroughly with a paper towel and store for future use. Some gourmets will place a small amount of oil on their fingertips to recoat their woks to keep them in top cooking condition.

Eventually, through repeated usage, a dark brown film will develop in the wok. The wok is now truly seasoned. This film is essentially carbon and is not harmful to one's health. The bottom of the wok, the part that touches the cooking flame of the stove, should definitely be scoured occasionally to free it of collected residue.

If one has the misfortune to accidentally burn food in the wok, it will be necessary to take steel wool and scour out the burned material and then reseason the wok once again. Each time that one has to scour out the wok with abrasive material, then one should reseason the wok.

Stainless steel woks sometimes stick when used to cook omelets or for stir-frying meats. To overcome this problem, one can spend five minutes to season the wok before use, or spray a coating of lecithin on the surface of the wok to allow for easy gliding of the foods. Lecithin is sold commercially under several brand names as "nonstick" cooking aids.

Wok Cooking Methods

Boiling: Boiling water, soups, dumplings, rice, blanching vegetable or noodles.

Braising: Braised dishes are commonly made using woks. Braising is useful when reducing sauces.

Deep Frying: Usually accomplished with larger woks to reduce splashing, but for deep frying of less food or small food items, small woks are also used: fried vermicelli noodles or sweet and sour chicken.

Pan Frying: Food that is fried using a small amount of oil in the bottom of a wok: pot stickers or omelets.

Roasting: Cooking food with dry heat in an enclosed wok with cover.

Searing: Food is carbonized on its outer surfaces by the application of high heat: salmon filet.

Smoking: Food can be hot smoked by putting the smoking material in the bottom of the wok while food is placed on a rack above.

Steaming: Done using a dedicated wok for boiling water in combination with steaming baskets: dumplings or fish.

Stewing: Woks are sometimes used for stewing, though it is more common in Chinese cuisine to use either stoneware or porcelain for such purposes, especially when longer stewing times are required.

Stir-Frying: Frying food quickly in a small amount of oil over high heat while stirring continuously.

Basting   Using no oil to toast; just heat: sesame seeds.

Safety and Care

Units with safety valves—lighting and shut down instructions:

Always follow these lighting and shutdown instructions when operating your unit.

A five-minute complete shutoff period is required before lighting or relighting pilot.

1. Check that all gas valves on the unit are turned off (lever handles in horizontal position) before turning on main gas line. Check for leaks using soapy water or other suitable leak detector.

Never Use Open Flame for Testing

1. Main burner valve should be in off position
2. Place a burning match by the pilot burner in the combustion chamber of the range.
3. Depress red safety pilot button on and light pilot.
4. The pilot should light. Continue to hold the button for 1 minute or until the pilot stays lit.

Temporary and Extended Shutdown

For temporary shutdown, turn all burner valves to off position.

For an extended period of time, turn all burner valves off and also turn off gas supply to the range.

Maintenance and Care

If equipment requires service, contact your authorized gas service company to perform necessary repairs.

- Check the flue riser monthly to be sure it is free of obstructions. Be sure to clean the air mixers and orifices of ring burners once a year. Jet and shield tip burners must be serviced more often as they become clogged more easily. This service must be performed by a qualified gas service company.
- The range should be cleaned each evening with grease dissolver and rinsed well. It will prevent grease accumulation and keep the unit clean and sanitary.
- If unit is supplied with casters, there should be a restraint on the appliance to limit its movement.
- If disconnection of the restraint becomes necessary, it is imperative that the restraint be reconnected after the appliance is returned to its originally installed position.

Additional Cleaning and Care

Buildup around small wok ring:

Carefully, with dry kitchen towels or hot hand mittens, remove cooled ring from its resting place. Turn the ring on its side and rest it on top of the burner. Turn the burner on high flame. Burn for five minutes or as needed until the coated buildup dissolves and turns to ashes. Repeat pattern throughout the ring until all buildup is dissolved to satisfaction. The process should take about twenty minutes, depending on the severity of the buildup on the ring.

Take extra precaution when turning the ring; it is extremely hot.

Buildup on jet and shield tip burners:

Use an emptied and cleaned #10 can. Remove label, bottom, and top of can. Flatten can completely. Turn burner valves to off position. Then, with the flattened can, place it flat directly on top of the shield tip burners. Turn burner valves on high. With constant supervision, allow the flames to burn for up to fifteen minutes. Turn burner valves to off position. Using long tongs and hot hand mittens, take the #10 can off the shield tip burners and allow to cool completely before storing it. **Take extra precaution when removing #10 can; it is extremely hot.**

Buildup on small or large woks:

Turn burner valves to off position. Then turn the wok on an angle to its side and allow it to rest on the ring. Turn burner valves on full blast. Burn for five minutes or as needed until the inside buildup dissolves and turns to ashes. Carefully, with dry kitchen towels or hot hand mittens, repeat pattern throughout the wok until all buildup is dissolved to satisfaction. The process should take about fifteen minutes, depending on the severity of buildup on the ring.

Take extra precaution when turning the wok; it is extremely hot.

Once the wok is completely burned off, position wok to its regular sitting position and wipe ashes out. Then wash and scrub with water and a stainless steel scrub only. Once the inside is cleaned, turn it upside down and scrub the bottom side with water and a stainless steel scrub only. Return wok to its normal resting place and season.

Wok Condiment Stand

Oyster sauce, master soy sauce, teriyaki sauce, pad Thai sauce, orange sauce, rice wine, sri racha, sesame oil, garlic minced in vinegar oil, ginger minced in vinegar oil, and cornstarch slurry

Dry chili pepper, dry orange peels, salt, white pepper, yellow curry powder, Korean powder, and black pepper

Fresh beaten whole eggs (iced), white vinegar, sugar, dashi, fish sauce, and soy sauce

Dry folded kitchen towels and tasting spoons

Wok Equipment

Carbon steel small wok—fourteen inches (with handle)—and large wok, eighteen inches or bigger (with ears)

Wok wooden-handled ladle and spatula

Dry kitchen towels

Stainless steel scrub (new)

Strainers; tennis racquet and double meshed basket

Skimmer

One-gallon stainless steel round bain-marie for oil

Two-gallon stainless steel round bain-marie for running water

Preparation Prior to Cooking

Always check to see if you have all the ingredients on hand before preparing meals.

Cut up your meat and vegetables, marinating any that require this process. Set aside for cooking. If you are cooking several wok dishes at the same meal, prepare all of them before cooking any.

Place oil in wok, heating until oil just begins to smoke.

Stir-fry your meat, onions, or garlic together. Then add other ingredients accordingly.

Preparation for Wok Training
Cornstarch Slurry
Ingredients:
1½ pounds cornstarch
5 cups water, cold (1 cup reserved)

Directions:
Preparation time: 2 minutes
1. Mix cornstarch and 4 cups of cold water together until dissolved.
2. Boil 1 cup of water in wok, turn off heat, and add 1 tablespoon of cornstarch slurry. Immediately mix thoroughly; do not allow clumping. This should be loose with a slight thickness. Tempering and mixing the hot cornstarch water into the cold cornstarch concentrate will make the cooking process easier and more efficient because there will be less settling and hardening of the cornstarch.

Beef Flank
Ingredients:
4 ounces vegetable oil
5 ounces beef flank (marinated and sliced for stir-fry)

Directions:
Cooking time: 45 seconds

1. Heat and season wok with 1 ounce oil.
2. Pour back oil into the remaining oil.
3. On medium high heat, put beef in wok.
4. Add all oil immediately and loosen beef.
5. Continue to agitate the oil by stirring the beef and rocking the wok.
6. Beef should be cooked tenderly and not be crispy or browning on the edges.
   Once beef is cooked, allow excess oil from beef to drain.

DID YOU KNOW?

Chili, *chile,* and *chilli* are all spellings that are recognized by a wide variety of dictionaries.

Chili is widely used, although in much of South America the plant and its fruit are better known as *ají*, *locoto*, *chile*, or *rocoto*.

Chile is an alternate usage, the most common Spanish spelling in Mexico, as well as some parts of the United States and Canada. In the American Southwest, *chile* also denotes a thick, spicy, unvinegared sauce, which is available in red and green varieties and is quite often served over numerous types of New Mexican cuisine.

Chilli was the original Romanization of the Náhuatl language word for the fruit and is the preferred British spelling, according to the *Oxford English Dictionary*, although it also lists *chile* and *chili* as variants.

Fried Rice
Yield: 1 Serving

Ingredients:

2 ounces vegetable oil

4 ounces eggs, beaten (2 whole eggs)

1 ounce green onion, fine diced (reserve ½ ounce for garnish)

1 ounce red bell pepper, fine diced

1 ounce red onion, fine diced

1 ounce carrots, shredded

2 ounces broccoli crowns, small cuts

1 ounce baby corn, ¼-inch cuts

1 ounce bean sprouts

16 ounces cooked jasmine rice (hot)

Pinch salt

1 ounce master soy sauce (2 parts soy sauce, 1 part oyster sauce, 1½ parts mushroom soy sauce, 1½ parts sugar)

1 tablespoon oyster sauce

1 teaspoon sesame oil, toasted

Directions:

Cooking time: 1½ minutes

- Heat and season wok with 2 ounces oil.
- On high heat, add eggs and gently scramble.
- Add all vegetables except bean sprouts and toss.
- Add rice and toss vigorously to loosen rice.
- Add salt and toss.
- Add master soy and oyster sauce. Toss to completely coat and loosen any remaining grains of rice.
- Add bean sprouts and toss.
- Add sesame oil; this should always be the last ingredient added, allowing the essence of the oil to freshly infuse with the dish.
- Serve in bowl and garnish with the reserved finely diced green onion.

Fried Beef Noodles
Yield: 1 Serving

Ingredients:

1 recipe pan fried noodles (see recipe)
5 oz beef flank sliced for stir fry (see recipe)
½ ounce vegetable oil
1 teaspoon garlic, minced
1 teaspoon ginger, minced
1 ounce bean sprouts
1 ounce baby bok choy
1 ounce baby corn, cut
1 ounce straw mushrooms
¼ ounce shiitake mushrooms
1 ounce red bell, julienned
5 ounces beef flank, sliced for stir-fry (see instructions)
1 teaspoon rice wine
2 ounces master soy sauce (2 parts soy sauce, 1 part oyster sauce, 1½ parts mushroom soy sauce, 1½ parts sugar)
1 tablespoon oyster sauce
9 ounces chicken stock
2 ounces cornstarch slurry (thickness will depend on cornstarch concentration; add more if needed)
1 teaspoon sesame oil, toasted

Directions
Cooking time: maximum of 1 minute

1. Place pan-fried noodles on serving plate. The rest of the ingredients will be placed on top later.
2. Heat and season wok with oil.
3. On medium heat, quickly brown garlic and ginger; do not let burn. Add all vegetables and beef into wok and toss. Then turn heat to high.
4. Add rice wine, master soy, and oyster sauce. Toss to completely coat meat and vegetables. This will infuse the sauces into the beef and vegetables.
5. Add chicken stock and let boil.
6. Add cornstarch slurry. Mix quickly and do not allow cornstarch to clump. Check for the desired thickness of the sauce. Add a little more cornstarch if needed.
7. Add sesame oil; this should always be the last ingredient added, allowing the essence of the oil to freshly infuse with the dish.
8. Turn off.
9. Gently, and one wok spoon at a time, top it over the pan-fried noodles. The sauce should penetrate through the center of the noodles. Continue this until all ingredients are placed on top of noodles. Sauce should not be loose and running nor thick and clumpy.
10. No garnish. Serve immediately.

Fried Noodles
Yield: 1 Serving

Ingredients:
4 ounces vegetable oil
4 ounces Cantonese egg noodles

Directions:
Cooking time: maximum of 2 minutes

1. Boil noodles (al dente). Set aside and drain, while preparing the wok.
2. Heat and season wok with ½ ounce of oil.
3. On medium high heat, add 2½ ounces of oil and immediately, gently place the noodles into the wok.
4. Wait 5 seconds to allow the noodles to set form, while gently pushing the edges of the noodles inward.
5. In a gentle and quick motion, swirl the noodles around the wok, allowing even distribution of heat to bottom side of the noodles. Continue this motion until bottom has an even color of toasted brown.
6. Drain excess oil into the remaining oil before frying the top side; place wok spoon over noodles while draining oil.
7. Place back on heat and carefully flip the noodles.
8. Add all the remaining oil to the wok. Repeat procedure 5.
9. Once both sides are fried, place noodles on paper to absorb any additional oil.
10. Pan fried noodles should be one solid piece; crispy on the outside and soft on the inside. Do not cover airtight when storing.

REVIEW QUESTIONS

1. The most widely known Chinese cuisines are _____ and _____.

2. The following type of wok needs seasoning:
   a   Iron
   b   Steel
   c   Stainless steel
   d   Both a & b

3. Never use these to clean a wok:
   a   Soap and bamboo brush
   b   Water and nylon scouring pads
   c   Both a & b

4. How many ingredients are on the condiment stand?
   a   16
   b   18
   c   21

5. Sri racha sauce from Thailand contains the following ingredients:
   a   Chili, lemon grass, vinegar, garlic and salt
   b   Chili, Sugar, lime juice, garlic and salt
   c   Chili, Sugar, vinegar, ginger and salt
   d   Chili, Sugar, vinegar, garlic and salt

6. Our signature sauce is:
   a   Dashi
   b   Sri racha Sauce
   c   Master soy sauce
   d   Hoisin sauce

7. These are cooking methods executed in the wok:
   a   Pan frying, roasting, and smoking
   b   Steaming, stewing, and toasting
   c   Broiling, boiling, and braising
   d   Both a and b

8. What spice is commonly referred to as "hot pepper," "pepper flower," or "wild pepper," even though it is not a true pepper?

9. The oil we use in wok cookery is:
   a   Cottonseed/canola blend
   b   Peanut oil
   c   Soybean
   d   Malaysian coconut

10. Slurry is made with these ingredients:
    a   Water and cornstarch
    b   Water and potato starch
    c   Water and rice flour

"A dessert without cheese is like a beautiful woman with only one eye."

Jean Anthelme Brillat-Savarin

14

CHEESE

Definition

Cheese is an ancient food. The origin predates recorded history; the earliest evidence of cheese making has been found in Egyptian tombs, dating to about 2000 BC. The earliest cheeses were likely to have been quite sour and salty, similar in texture to rustic cottage cheese and feta. The Romans began to make hard cheeses for their legionnaires' supplies.

Wisconsin has garnered more cheese-making awards than any other state or country in the world and leads the nation in production. The cheese-making tradition of Wisconsin includes favorite cheeses such as Colby and Cheddar. Specialty cheeses, such as Asiago, Gouda, and Gorgonzola, keep up with consumer appetites for gourmet foods.

At the Casino, we began making fresh cheese as part of the Culinary Academy with great success, and various restaurants are now incorporating some of these cheeses into their menus.

The selection of fresh cheeses, handcrafted from hormone free milk and cream, include:
- Whole milk ricotta
- Mozzarella
- Ricotta salada
- Triple cream mascarpone
- Quark

Milk—what is it?

Fresh milk from the healthy animal is about as good as it gets. It contains its own system of cultures and enzymes that make it suited for the newly born and young as well as for cheese making.

The physical makeup of this milk is primarily:
- *Water* (88 percent)
- *Lactose* (4.5–5.5 percent), the milk sugar which serves as fuel for the lactic bacteria
- *Protein* (3.5 percent in cows to over 8 percent in ewes), primarily the casein for cheese structure
- *Fat* (3.5–5 percent in cows up to 9 percent for ewes), providing flavor, aroma, and texture in cheese
- *Minerals*, such as calcium, which form the casein bonds for cheese
- *Enzymes*, such as lipase and plasmin, which aid in the ripening of cheese

These components in fresh milk are kept in suspension due to the nature of the casein particle (milk's primary protein), and these in turn trap the fat particles. This suspended particle condition will later be altered in cheese making via rennet, acidity, and heat.

It is this change in the casein structure which causes the white fluid milk to form into the firm jell which becomes the curd of our developing cheese.

This process can be either a controlled development of positive lactic bacteria populations (as in cheese making), or it can be the wild growth of wild bacteria that will simply result in the souring of the milk.

This quality and balance of milk components also make possible the wonderful array of cheeses due to differing breeds, diets, seasons, and even geographic areas.

What can go wrong with it?

From the moment that the milk leaves the animal's udder, things begin to change.

First, as the milk leaves its healthy environment it enters a much harsher environment of possible contamination. It is here that the milk producer has a great ability to control the quality of milk by preparing and keeping a clean milking area and practicing a proper sanitation routine.

Next, in commercial milking, as the milk moves through the tubes, pipes, and pumps into the refrigerated tanks, more physical changes begin to take place: Fat globules can be damaged, releasing enzymes that can cause problems in ripening.During long cold storage, more of the calcium can go into solution, resulting in weak curds.Also, during cold storage certain undesirable bacteria that grow well at these cold temperatures can increase to very large populations.

Finally, as the milk is transported and then cold stored again, the above problems begin to accelerate.

Since the lactose in milk is a very good food supply for many types of microbes, all of the above conditions translate into a deteriorating milk quality. This makes it important to preserve this milk for the public in a safe manner.

What is being done to accomplish this?

In 1857 Louis Pasteur realized that heat treatment would destroy unwanted microbes, and shortly after this the pasteurization of milk began in Europe and America. By 1940 this process became well established as dairy herds became larger, bulking milk became popular, milk travelled farther, and larger milk processing plants and cheese factories held milk longer. There are several different approaches that will result in changing milk's quality:

Thermization or heat treatment

This is a low temperature (145°F) and short (fifteen seconds) treatment that has the lowest impact on natural bacteria and enzymes in milk and is commonly practiced in Europe.

Pasteurization can take one of two forms:

Low temperature (145°F), long time (thirty minutes)

High temperature (162°F), short time (fifteen seconds)

At either of these points, many of the enzymes and cultures are affected and calcium damage has become apparent, but the use of calcium chloride may reverse the latter. Dairy technicians have tried to replace the enzymes and cultures through science, but we all know that it is very hard to do as well as "Mother Nature."

One of the real downsides to pasteurization is that fresh milk naturally contains healthy bacteria that inhibit the growth of undesirable and dangerous organisms. Without these friendly bacteria, pasteurized milk is more susceptible to contamination.

We have all been led to believe that milk is a wonderful source of calcium, when in fact pasteurization diminishes the nutrient value of milk, making calcium and other minerals unavailable. Complete destruction of phosphatase is one method of testing to see if milk has been adequately pasteurized. Phosphatase is essential for the absorption of calcium.

Ultra pasteurization

This is a range of milk-processing temps from 191°-212°F for varying times

Once the temp rises above 174°F, the calcium component of the milk will be damaged to the point that a curd will not develop properly. If your curd forms as a loose mass or something looking like ricotta, then your milk source has been probably ultra pasteurized.

How to Make Mozzarella Cheese
Yield: 1 –1 ½ pound

Ingredients:
¼ tablet rennet
Water—chlorine free!
1½ teaspoons citric acid (you may need more if you use farm-fresh milk)
1 gallon milk

Equipment:
1 gallon stainless steel pot
Thermometer
Wire whisk, knife, and skimmer
Colander

Directions:
1. Dissolve ¼ tablet rennet in ¼ cup of cool water.
2. Mix 1½ teaspoons citric acid with 8 ounces cool water until dissolved, and then pour into your pot.
3. Pour milk into the pot and stir vigorously.
4. Heat the milk slowly to 90°F while stirring.*
5. Remove the pot from the burner and slowly stir in the rennet solution with up and down motions for approximately 30 seconds.
6. Cover the pot and leave it undisturbed for 5 minutes.
7. Check the curd. It should look like custard, with a clear separation between the curd and whey (see picture).
   **If the curd is too soft or the whey is milky, let set for a few more minutes.
   **If your milk did not form a curd, refer to "Choose Your Milk" (below).
8. Cut the curd with a knife that reaches to the bottom of your pot. See diagram.
9. Place the pot back on the stove and heat to 105°F while slowly moving the curds around with the spoon. Note: If you are stretching the curds with the water bath method, heat the curds to 110°F.
10. Take off the burner and continue to stir slowly for 2–5 minutes. (More time will make a firmer cheese.)
11. With a skimmer or slotted spoon, transfer the curd to a colander or bowl.
12. Put on your gloves; drain as much whey from the curd as you can, and transfer your curd to a micro-waveable bowl.
13. Place the bowl in the microwave and heat for 1 minute.
14. Remove and drain more whey as you gently fold the curds into one piece. Add 1 teaspoon salt (optional).
15. Microwave for another 30 seconds. Drain and stretch the curd. It must be 135°F to stretch properly. If it isn't hot enough, microwave for another 30 seconds.
16. Stretch the cheese by pulling like taffy until it is smooth and shiny. The more you work the cheese, the firmer it will be. Taste it°–yum! J
17. Now you can shape it into a log, ball, bite-size morsels (bocconcini), or braid.
18. When finished, submerge it in 50°F water to cool for 5 minutes and then in ice water. The cheese will hold its shape.

This step is critical, as it protects the silky texture and keeps it from becoming grainy.

Note: If using unpasteurized milk, add rennet at 88°F and do not heat over 90°F in step 9.

This will keep your cheese nice and moist.

You may also need to let the milk set in step 6 for up to 10 minutes.

You can store this for up to 2 weeks, Saran wrapped or in airtight container.

You can freeze it and reheat when ready to use.

You can store the curds and stretch them in a few days.

Choose Your Milk

This recipe works for cow, goat, dry powder, whole, and skimmed milk.

Use organic or hormone-free milk whenever possible.

If you can, buy local farm-fresh milk.

Ultra pasteurized does not work here.

Note:

Always use all nonreactive, stainless steel, glass, or ceramic equipment for cheese making.

DID YOU KNOW?

Ovolini (egg size): 4-ounce balls

Bocconcini (bite size): 1.50-ounce balls

Ciliegine (little cherry size): 0.33-ounce balls

Manteca is mozzarella molded around a lump of butter.

Burata is like a mozzarella truffle—a "skin" of mozzarella surrounding a mozzarella cream.

You can substitute with fresh mozzarella.

How to Make Ricotta Cheese
Yield: 1¾–2 pounds

Ingredients:
1 teaspoon citric acid (you may need more if you use farm-fresh milk)
Water—chlorine free!
1 gallon milk
1 teaspoon cheese salt (optional)

Equipment:
Always use all nonreactive, stainless steel, glass, or ceramic equipment for cheese making.

1 gallon stainless steel pot
Thermometer
Muslin cloth

Directions:
1. Mix 1 teaspoon citric acid with 8 ounces cool water until dissolved, and then pour into your pot.
2. Pour milk into the pot (add salt, optional). Stir.
3. Heat milk to 195°F—stir often to avoid scorching.
4. When the curds and whey separate, turn off the heat and let set for 5 minutes.
5. Line a colander with the cheesecloth.
6. Ladle the curds gently into the cloth.
7. Tie the cloth into a bag and hang to drain for ½ hour or more, depending on the desired consistency.
8. After draining, the cheese is ready to eat. J

NOTE:
Cheese will keep for up to two weeks, or it may be frozen.

ix 1 tsp citric acid with 8 oz cool water until dissolved.

Pour citric acid mixture into your pot.

Slowly pour milk into your pot.

ace your pot on burner and stir.

Heat milk to 195°F – stir often to avoid scorching.

Remove from the burner once the curds & whey separate.

emove from heat, cover and let set for 5 minutes.

Gently ladle the curds from the pot.

Ladle curds into a colander lined with cheese cloth.

Tie the cloth into a bag.

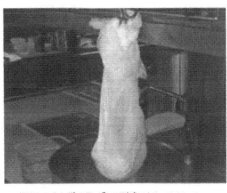

Hang to drain for ½ hour or more, depending on desired consistency.

After draining, the cheese is ready to eat. It will keep for up to two weeks or it may be frozen.

Pumpkin Quark Cheesecake
Yield: 1 cake for 12 servings

Ingredients:
16 ounces   quark cream cheese
1 cup brown sugar
24 ounces   roasted pumpkin, pureed
Zest from 1 orange
½ teaspoon ground cinnamon
½ teaspoon ground ginger
½ teaspoon ground nutmeg
4 eggs
¼ teaspoon salt

Preparation:
1. Preheat oven to 350ºF (175ºC).
2. Beat together the cheese and the sugar until smooth.
3. Add the pumpkin, orange zest, and the spices (cinnamon, ginger, and nutmeg).
4. Beat in eggs one at a time.
5. Add salt and beat until creamy.
6. Pour the batter evenly into a cake pan with the crust prepared (recipe below).
7. Bake for 50 minutes or until the knife inserted in the center comes out clean.
8. Let cool.

Graham Crust Ingredients:
1 cup graham cracker crumbs
½ cup butter, melted
¼ cup brown sugar

Graham Crust Preparation:
1. Combine all ingredients.
2. Spread evenly in the baking pan for base.

> **NOTE:**
> *Pumpkin may be replaced with other fruit.*

DID YOU KNOW?

Quark is a type of fresh cheese. It's made by warming soured milk until the desired degree of denaturation of milk proteins is met. Then it's strained. Dictionaries usually translate "quark cheese" as baker's cheese or cottage cheese, although most commercial varieties of cottage cheese are made with rennet, whereas traditional quark is not. Quark is soft and white, similar to some types of fresh cheese. It is distinct from ricotta because ricotta is made from scalded milk. It is quite similar to the Indian cheese paneer. Quark usually has no salt added and is often used as an ingredient for pastries, sandwiches, and salads throughout Europe. Lately, its popularity is the United States has been growing.

REVIEW QUESTIONS:

1. What is curdling?

2. True or false: Ultra pasteurized milk does not work with this recipe.

3. This aging period (also called ripening, or, from the French, affinage) is how long?
   a   One day to week
   b   One week to month
   c   A few days to several years

4. True or false: As a cheese ages, microbes and enzymes transform texture and intensify flavor.

5. What is rennet?

6. What function does rennet have in cheese making?

7. What is the nutritional value of cheese?

8. The top cheese-producing country is:
   United States
   Germany
   France

9. This country has the top per capita consumption of cheese:
   Greece   68.4 pounds
   France   57.4 pounds
   Iceland   55.9 pounds
   US   33 pounds, up from 11 pounds in 1970

10. Explain whey or milk serum.

11. What effect does pasteurization have?

12. This is America's favorite cheese (one third of the annual per capita consumption):
    Mozzarella
    American
    Cheddar

"Teamwork is the fuel that allows common people to attain uncommon results."

Andrew Carnegie

15

CURE

Charcuterie is the art of making sausages and other cured, smoked, and preserved meats. In addition to sausages, classic items also include pâtés, terrines, galantines, ballotines, and crèpinettes. Charcuterie is one of the principal categories of *garde manger*, which encompasses various classical techniques for preserving foods that date from an era before refrigeration.Originally, the word *charcuterie* was used to refer only to products made from pork. But today, the word *charcuterie* is used to describe any product prepared using these traditional methods, even ones made from poultry, fish, seafood, or other meats.One of the characteristics of charcuterie recipes is their use of forcemeat. But familiar smoked or cured meats, such as ham and bacon, are technically within the purview of charcuterie.

Curing and brining are among the most popular methods of preserving meats, poultry, and fish. At one time hard curing was the only method used to preserve meat. The meat was packed in a container with just salt. Over a period of several days, the salt would draw moisture out of the meat, producing a brine. The liquid was drained off. More salt was added, and the process was repeated until the meat was hard and dry. The final product would keep indefinitely but had to be soaked in fresh water several times to get rid of the salt before it was edible.
Curing and brining are regaining importance in the kitchen again, more often used to add flavor and texture to meat.

Curing is a dry process. It can take from hours to months. To add flavor when curing, one may use herbs, spices, and items like maple sugar and molasses. All of these items add depth to the flavor of the product, not just a salty effect.
Most products are smoked after curing.

Brining is a wet process, in which we basically take a cure and add water to it to create a saline or curing solution. The product needs to be immersed in brine; when you brine items, they usually will take a shorter period of time to cure as opposed to dry curing items. A portion of the brine may also be injected into the product.

Parma Ham
Making a Parma ham is a long and painstaking process. The curing is controlled carefully so that the ham absorbs only enough salt to preserve it. By the end, a trimmed ham will have lost more than a quarter of its weight through moisture loss, helping to concentrate the flavor. The meat becomes tender and the distinctive aroma and flavor of *prosciutto di Parma* emerge. Prosciutto is made from the ham (hind leg or thigh) of either a pig or wild boar. The process of making prosciutto can take anywhere from three months to two years, depending on the size of the ham.
For centuries, Parma ham has been prized for its enticing aroma and incomparable flavor. By law this famous ham can be made and cured only in the gently rolling countryside near Parma, Italy.

Four ingredients are essential to the production of *prosciutto di Parma*: Italian pigs, salt, air, and time.
Prosciutto di Parma is an all-natural ham; additives such as sugar, spices, smoke, water, and nitrites are prohibited.

"Despite the economic turmoil and challenging Environment facing everyone in the industry, I believe That with focus on quality and service, team member Development and training, and being "locked on" to our Guests' needs, we will stay the course and be able to Operate successfully in our exciting industry."

Omnivore's Travel

Smoked Bacon
Yield: 10 pounds

Ingredients:
1 fresh pork belly, about 10 pounds
9 ounces kosher salt
7 ounces brown sugar
1 ounce TCM

Preparation:
1. Weigh pork belly and adjust the cure as needed.
2. For the cure, mix the dry ingredients well.
3. Rub the cure onto the belly, making sure to cover the belly entirely.
4. Place in a plastic tub with the skin side down.
5. Cure in the refrigerator for 21 days, turning every day. Keep it covered.
6. Rinse the belly with water.
7. Soak for at least 1 hour in fresh water.
8. Hot smoke at 120ºF–170ºF to an internal temperature of 150ºF (approximately 4 hours).
9. Cool, wrap in plastic, and refrigerate.
10. Slice as needed, with or without the rind.

> **NOTE:**
> *Cut the belly to fit the curing container or smoke chamber.*
> *You may also use the belly unsmoked, popular in Germany and Korea.*

DID YOU KNOW?

Tinted curing mixture, or TCM, is a curing mixture composed of 6.25 percent sodium nitrite and 93.75 percent table salt. It's used in making cured meat products like sausages and corned beef. TCM functions as a food preservative, and it also has antimicrobial properties. The pink coloring is added so that it won't be mistaken for ordinary salt. It is responsible for producing the pink color in cured meats such as hot dogs and corned beef. Also known as Prague Powder No. 1, curing salt, and pink salt, one teaspoon mixed with cold water will cure about five pounds of meat. Another special property of TCM is that it prevents the growth of the deadly *Clostridium botulinum* bacteria, which causes botulism.

Choose Your Wood

Wood selection for smoking is an important factor.

The resin present in the wrong types creates undesirable color and aroma and even bitter flavor.

Avoid cedar, cypress, elm, eucalyptus, pine, fir, redwood, sassafras, spruce, and sycamore.

Good choices are the following:

Apple is very mild in flavor and gives food sweetness. This is good with poultry and pork. Apple will discolor chicken skin (turns it dark brown).

Hickory adds a strong flavor to meats, so be careful not to use too excessively. It's good with beef and lamb.

Maple, like fruit wood, gives a sweet flavor that is excellent with poultry and ham.

Mesquite has been very popular of late and is good for grilling, but since it burns hot and fast, it's not recommended for long barbecues. Mesquite is probably the strongest flavored wood; hence its popularity with restaurant grills that cook meat for a very short time.

Oak is strong but not overpowering, a very good wood for beef or lamb, and the most versatile hardwood.

Pecan burns cool and provides a delicate flavor. It's a much subtler version of hickory.

Plum is great for poultry and pork, similar to hickory but milder in flavor.

Walnut has a heavy, smoky flavor and should be mixed with milder flavored woods.

Other good choices: avocado, bay, chestnut, fig, guava, olive, and willow.

Italian Bacon (Pancetta)
Yield: 10 pounds

Ingredients:
1 fresh pork belly, about 10 pounds
9 ounces kosher salt
2 ounces crushed juniper berries
2 ounces cracked black peppercorn
2 ounces brown sugar
4 small bay leaves, crushed
4 garlic cloves, crushed
1 ounce TCM

Preparation:
1. Weigh pork belly and adjust the cure as needed (8 ounces of cure for 10 pounds).
2. For the cure, mix the dry ingredients well.
3. Rub the cure onto the belly, making sure to cover the belly entirely.
4. Place in a plastic tub with the skin side down.
5. Cure in the refrigerator for 21 days, turning every day. Keep it covered.
6. Rinse the belly with water; remove the skin (can be used for cooking other dishes).
7. Roll into a cylinder and wrap with cheesecloth, tied tightly.
8. Hang to air dry for 3 weeks in a cool and dry area (50°F to 60°F with 60 to 65 percent humidity).
9. Cool, wrap in plastic, and refrigerate.
10. Slice as needed, with or without the rind.

> **NOTE:**
> *Cut the belly to fit the curing container or smoke chamber.*

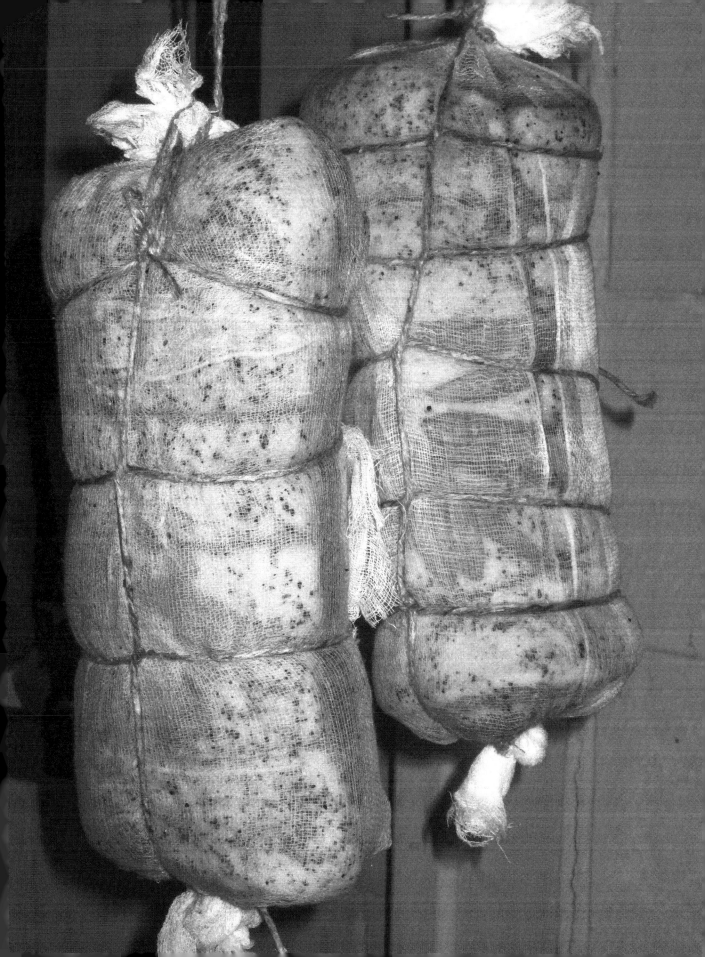

REVIEW QUESTIONS

1. What types of sausages do we know?

2. What types of casings are used in sausage making?

3. What is green bacon?

4. Describe a traditional galantine?

5. Describe a traditional ballotine?

6. What other names are there for TCM?

7. Give another special property of TCM.

8. What is forcemeat?

9. What is panada?

10. What is salumi?

DID YOU KNOW?

Garde manger (pronunciation: gard man-ZHAY) refers to a category of foods produced in the cold kitchen, for example:

- Cured and smoked foods
- Salads and dressings
- Sausages, pâtés, and terrines
- Pickled foods
- Cold soups and sauces
- Cheeses

Garde manger means "keeping to eat" in French, and the term originally referred to a pantry or food storage area.In the modern culinary arts, the term *garde manger* can refer to the chef who oversees cold food production.

Certificate of Completion

This certificate is awarded to

Brenda Wallenkamp

In recognition of completion of the

Culinary Academy

on September 17, 2007

9/17/2007

Peter Gebauer, GMC Executive Chef

Date

"If your actions inspire others to dream more, learn more, do more, and become more, you are a leader."

John Quincy Adams, US President

16

ANSWERS AND TESTING

1 KNIVES ANSWERS
1. The chef's knife or French knife is considered the most versatile knife.
2. A paring knife is generally used for trimming fruits and vegetables.
3. A filet knife is more flexible than a boning knife.
4. The tip is used for fine cuts, the middle is used for chopping and slicing, and the heel is used for cutting through bones and joints.
5. The purpose of the bolster/collar is to serve as a barrier between the hand and blade.
6. The tang is the metal part of the knife that extends into the handle.
7. A dull knife is dangerous due to the possibility of it slipping and cutting the user.
8. The material that is used to sharpen the knife must be stronger than the knife.
9. A knife should be steeled after it has been sharpened on a stone.
10. When steeling the knife, one should always begin with the heel.
11. After steeling a knife, it should always be wiped clean with either soap and water or vinegar
12. A knife should always be passed by the handle.
13. Cross-contamination is when undesirable elements are passed from one food to another.
14. When choosing a way to store and transport your knives, one should always be aware of safety and sanitation.
15. One should clean one's knives after use and between significant tasks.
16. *Chiffonade,* or shredding leafy vegetables or herbs, means to cut parallel very fine with a French knife.
17. The two types of *mirepoix* are the basic and the white.
18. *Matignon,* or edible *mirepoix*, consists of onions, carrots, celery, pork (ham, bacon, or lard), and thyme.

2 SAUTÉ ANSWERS

1. Tender cuts of meat, fish, and poultry.
2. The main product, fat (the searing agent), and liquids for deglazing.
3. Flavoring (herbs, spices, condiments, liqueurs); finishing (butter, cream, glace); garnishing.
4. A sauté pan (*sauteuse* or *sautoir*) is best. These pans are the appropriate size and made out of the appropriate type of metal to allow for high heat and to minimize accumulation of moisture. Deep pans, for example, may allow too much moisture to accumulate, which will ruin the item being sautéed.
5. Preheat the pan; make sure the item is absolutely dry; do not overcrowd the pan with too many items; do not overcook.
6. The item will release its juices, which will boil, causing the item to become tough.
7. This sears the outside of the main item, creating a uniform, thin coating which aids in proper color, protects the flesh, and seals in the juices of the item.
8. If the item is not completely dry, the moisture will cause it to spatter when placed in the pan, which may injure the chef. In addition, moisture will cause the main item to become tough.
9. The high heat aids in searing the main item, which creates a coating and seals in the juices.
10. Once. If the item is turned too many times, it will overcook. Sautéing is a quick cooking method. Using the proper cut of meat, fish, or poultry (tender) will make it unnecessary to turn the item more than once.
11. By touch and by color of the coating.
12. After the item is cooked, the excess fat is poured off. The pan is returned to medium heat, being careful not to burn the fond. Add the garniture and sauté lightly, then add the liquid and scrape up the bits of fond. Cream or glace may be added at this time along with any herbs. Taste the sauce and make sure that it is seasoned properly.
13. It is usually accompanied by a butter-based sauce, such as *meuniere*.
14. Because sautéing fish does not create any useable fond, while red meat and poultry do.
15. Wine, stock, sauce bases, and liquors.
16. Butter, cream, and glace.
17. No, because they are *a la minute* items that are served immediately after they are cooked. This is because they are portion-cut items that could either become overcooked easily by heating again or from carryover cooking, or they can become tough and unappealing if cooked twice.

3 FRY ANSWERS

1. Pan frying and deep fat frying are high heat, dry cooking methods. Liquid fat is the cooking medium used either in a pan or a deep fat fryer. Items used for frying are often coated with bread crumbs.
2. Crisp brown exterior and moist tender interior.
3. A procedure in which an item is dipped in flour, then an egg wash of eggs and milk, cream, or water, then dredged in bread crumbs or batter. This process will create the coating from frying.
4. False. The temperature must be at least 350 degrees. If the temperature is too low, fat will be absorbed into the item, making it greasy and soggy. A crisp brown crust will not be created.
5. To create crisp brown crust, to ensure that the crust adheres to the item, to thoroughly cook the item without burning it.
6. Trim the meat of all fat and any silver skin. Pat dry.
7. Overcrowding can create moisture, which will result in a soggy product. It causes the temperature to drop and the items will not form a food seal.
8. Clean and trim item, pat dry, and season. Dredge in flour, then egg wash, then batter or bread crumbs. Place a corner of the item into the hot oil and when it begins to cook, gently let go of the item. It should float.
9. Salt away from the fryer to avoid contamination of the oil.
10. Drain and filter the oil after each shift. Turn the heat down when not in use. Clean during service by skimming out any particles.
11. If the fat smells and/or smokes at low temperatures.
12. Any excess moisture can result in a soggy product rather than a crisp one.
13. They will stick. They also may become soggy; some of the breading may fall off.
14. Briefly drain on absorbent paper towels to drain off any excess fat.
15. It shimmers, or has haze over the surface.

4. BRAISE ANSWERS

1. Braising benefits less tender cuts of meat by making them more tender and flavorful.
2. The pot should have a tight-fitting lid to assure proper moisture retention and reduce shrinkage.
3. Lard might be necessary if the cut of meat is deficient in fat or marbleization.
4. The meat is dried to help in caramelization and prevent the spitting and spattering that can occur as a result of surface moisture.
5. The meat should be placed in the oil fat side down.
6. The liquid should not be allowed to boil in the braising process because this can lead to shrinkage and drying, and the sauce will appear unclear.
7. The meat should be turned occasionally to prevent drying and assure even cooking.
8. The process of *degrassier* is allowing the fat to come to the surface of the sauce so it can be removed.
9. *Depouillage* is when the sauce is returned to the pot and allowed to simmer so additional fat and impurities can be skimmed off until it is clear.
10. To thicken the sauce, any of the following can be added: roux, modified starches, potatoes, gingersnaps, bread crumbs, or blood.
11. A braised piece of meat should be sliced against the grain.
12. Marinating can tenderize and reduce any game flavors in the meat.
13. One can tell when the meat is done by inserting a fork into the meat. If it is easy to remove, it is done.
14. For every pound of meat, six to ten ounces of cooking liquids should be used.
15. Common cooking liquids can include stocks, water, beer, wine, and marinades.
16. The three options for preparing the sauce are:

    - After searing the product, deglaze the pan and add a light consistency brown sauce.
    - After searing the product, add flour to the fat used to sear, and then add liquid.
    - After cooking the product, reduce the cooking liquid and then thicken.

17. The minimum holding temperature for braised meat is 135°F.
18. The proper way of holding a braised item is:
    a   Hold large pieces in a small amount of stock to keep moist.
    b   Hold at below 41°F or above 135°F.

5 BROIL AND GRILL ANSWERS

1. Broiling and grilling are high heat cooking methods, reserved for tender, portion-size cuts of meat, fish, poultry, and vegetables. The items are cooked close to radiant heat. In grilling, the heat source is below the item; in broiling, it is above the item.

2. No. Grilling and broiling are *a la minute* cooking methods. The items cooked must be tender in the raw state; the cooking method is too brief to tenderize a tough item.

3. Clean the chicken, trim excess fat. Remove wings. Cut end of leg joint and partially cut through leg joint. Marinate. Heat hinged grill; clean with wire brush. Oil grids with towel. Place chicken on the grill, close clamp. Place grill in hottest spot to mark until "dore." Remove bones. Place in oven to complete cooking process.

4. Trim excess fat. Marinate if desired, or brush with oil. Place steak at angle on grids. Check for grill marks with offset spatula. Turn steak 180 degrees to create alternate grill marks. Turn steak if preparing for immediate service. Continue cooking until desired doneness. Determine doneness with finger pressure method.

5. High heat creates the grill marks characteristic of grilling and broiling. It also prevents the item from sticking to the grates.

6. To prevent the item from sticking, and to prevent flavor from residue of previously grilled items from penetrating the item being grilled.

7. Baking soda; sheet pan to cover flame.

8. Finger test; gently press with fingertips. The greater the resistance, the more well done the item is. Visual testing is not reliable.

9. To prevent a smoky kitchen and minimize fire hazard.

10. With the use of high heat, oil on the grids, and marinade in the item being grilled.

11. No. Grilled vegetables do not retain their heat, and therefore should be served immediately.

12. High, medium, low. The high heat is used first, to allow the grill marks to be created. An item may be moved to a medium temperature zone, after the grill marks have been formed, to complete the cooking process. This will also make room for new items to be placed on the grill.

13. A wire brush is used to clean the grids, removing any leftover food particles from previously grilled items.

14. Broiled and grilled foods do not require sauces or flavorings, which often add calories and or sodium. During the cooking process, the fat in the item melts off into the heat source, which leaves the item less fatty. It also creates smoke, which imparts the unique flavor the items.

15. The heat source will most likely flare up, possibly causing a fire.

16. Wash and trim vegetables. Cut into thick slices at an angle. Marinate briefly. Heat, clean, and oil the grill. Place vegetables on grill, at an angle. Once the first grill marks have been made, turn the items to complete the grill pattern. Turn the item over. Gently touch to check for doneness.

6 POACH AND STEAM ANSWERS

1. Poaching is a moist cooking method.
2. Very little liquid is used, just enough to cover the food item.
3. Excessive heat during poaching will cause the meat to become dry and stringy.
4. Doneness of a food item can be checked both visually and by touch.
5. Deep poaching would be used instead of shallow poaching to produce a firmer finished product.
6. If the food is very presentable, the sauce should be placed under the item to show off the excellence of the food. If it is not presentable, the sauce should be placed over the item.
7. Steaming is a moist cooking method.
8. During steaming, the liquid is brought to a boil.
9. The level of the liquid during steaming should always be kept beneath the food item.
10. During steaming, a hard boil should be used for larger, thicker food items to produce a more penetrating steam.
11. Steaming would be used instead of poaching when you don't want to lose any of the food item's original flavors or juices.
12. If you want to infuse flavor into an item, poaching would be used.

7 BOIL AND BLANCH ANSWERS

1. The product, the cooking medium, and the optional components.
2. To ensure uniform cooking and doneness.
3. Used for soups or stocks, purees, or compost if unusable.
4. Water and stock.
5. No. In order to keep the water at a boil and the temperature even, add the vegetables a little at a time.
6. Addition of milk to the cooking medium.
7. Red vegetables. This helps set the color.
8. Variety of seasonings and aromatics, wine, vinegar, herbs such as parsley.
9. It will cause the broccoli to discolor.
10. False. Some vegetables benefit from being covered, such as red and white vegetables. Green vegetables should not be covered, as trapping the moisture in will cause the vegetables to discolor. It may also exaggerate strong flavors and aromas.
11. When the average cooking time has passed, remove a test piece of the vegetable. Check for flavor and tenderness.
12. Blanching does not fully cook the vegetable. It can be used to remove the skins from tomatoes, eliminate or reduce strong odors or flavors, to set the color of vegetables to be used cold, or as a first step in other preparations, such as sauté of mixed vegetables.
13. When you want to use the vegetables in another dish, such as pan-fried zucchini.
14. Parboiling is similar to blanching, but cooks the vegetable a little longer than in blanching, although the vegetable is not fully cooked.
15. The vegetable will discolor.
16. Not all vegetables need to be cut prior to boiling. It depends on the type of vegetable and the intended use. Beets are often cooked whole.

8 STOCKS ANSWERS

1. Bones, *mirepoix*, *sachet d'epices*, tomato paste, oil, water.
2. Fleshy bones, minimal fat. The fleshiness imparts good flavor. Fat will cloud the stock and make it cloudy. Fresh, not frozen, will impart a better flavor. Approximately four inches in length. Knucklebones should not be used because they are too big and hard to cut.
3. Stockpot (tall and narrow), French and paring knives, spoon, ladle, skimmer, chinois, china cap, cheese-cloth, wooden paddle.
4. This flavoring "bag" is made out of cheesecloth and filled with peppercorns, thyme, bay leaf, parsley stems, and garlic. It is placed in the stock to add flavor to it.
5. Tall and narrow stainless steel pots. This is important because it makes it easier to skim off impurities and minimizes the evaporation of liquid during the cooking process, because the cooking area is small.
6. The celery has such high water content that the moisture would be released while browning the *mirepoix*, which would impede the caramelization process.
7. False. Rapidly boiling stocks will cause the stock to be cloudy. Stocks should cook at a lazy bubble.
8. Remove the pot from the heat. Use a china cap lined with dampened cheesecloth. Place it over a stainless steel pot and ladle the hot stock into the china cap to strain into the second stockpot.
9. Place a stainless steel rack in the bottom of the sink. This will allow the cold water to get under the stockpot. Surround with ice and fill sink with water till the level equals that of the stock. Stir periodically. This will ensure that the stock cools properly, minimizing the chance of bacterial growth.
10. Gather *mise en place*. Condition pan. Brown the bones. Add onions and carrots to caramelize. Add tomato paste. Deglaze the pan. Cover with water. Simmer for three hours. Remove impurities. Add sachet. Simmer one more hour. Strain, cool, and store.
11. Six hours, eight hours, three hours.
12. Eight pounds bones, six quarts water, one pound mirepoix.
13. Select bones (chicken, veal, and beef). Add liquid. Simmer for three hours. Add *mirepoix* and simmer. Add the sachet for the last hour of cooking. Strain, cool, and store.
14. Bones and trimmings (no gills), *mirepoix*, liquids (water, lemon juice, white wine), and aromatics.
15. Bones and trimmings of white-meat fish, such as turbot, sole, or flounder. Oily-fleshed fish are not suited for stocks. Gills must be removed as they impart a bitter flavor.
16. Soup, sauces, poaching liquid, glazes, stews, and consommé.

9 ROAST ANSWERS

1. Roasting is a dry cooking method.
2. The meat should be placed fat side up so the melting fats can help baste the meat while it roasts.
3. A smaller cut should be seared prior to roasting to caramelize the outer surface because cooking time is not sufficient enough to allow for browning.
4. *Mirepoix* is used during the roasting process to contribute flavor to the natural gravies derived from the drippings.
5. The *mirepoix* should be added thirty to forty minutes before the roast is due to be removed from the oven.
6. Carryover cooking is the cooking that continues to take place after the roast has been removed from the oven. It usually adds another five to fifteen degrees to the meat.
7. Trussing is the act of tying the meat item to help in shape, assist in carving, and heat distribution
8. The roast should be removed five to fifteen degrees before the desired temperature is reached.
9. The roast should be resting twenty to thirty minutes to allow for the juices that have concentrated in the center to redistribute as the muscle relaxes.
10. The roast should be held at a temperature above 135°F.
11. The two additional methods for checking for doneness with poultry are the twisting of the leg joint and raising the poultry, inserting a fork into the cavity, and making sure the juices "run clear."
12. Cornstarch is not the preferred thickening agent because it will make the sauce appear cloudy and give it a less desirable texture.
13. When cooking poultry, the drippings that are left in the pan are comprised of juice, fond, and fat.
14. Fond is the basis of the *jus* or pan gravy.
15. Basting should be done with the melted fat that has been extruded from the roasted item.
16. Nonfatty fowl can be brushed with melted butter or oil to help with the caramelization.

10. COST CONTROL ANSWERS

1. From 104 to 117 ounces.
2. The number of scoops yielded in a quart.
3. Two gallons or 256 ounces.
4. Sixty-four scoops.
5. Three.
6. Forty-eight or seventy-two cans.
7. Make banana bread.
8. Bread pudding, croutons, or bread crumbs.
9. Bacon
10. Labor, COGS, other expenses.
11. 1, Temperature at which meat is cooked.
    2, Internal temperature of the meat.
12. 1, Age of the meat—older meat cooks faster, shrinks more.
    2, Internal temperature prior to cooking—frozen vs. chilled.
    3, Desired degree of doneness—higher temperature equals longer cooking time.
    4, Quality and quantity of the protein.

11 SUSTAINABILITY ANSWERS

1. Confined Animal Feeding Operations. Highly mechanized operations designed to produce food cheaply and conveniently, there is growing recognition that factory farming creates a host of problems, including animal stress and abuse, pollution, and unnecessary use of hormones.

2. It is the process of transferring specific traits, or genes, from one organism into a different plant or animal. Genetic engineering is different from traditional cross breeding, where genes can only be exchanged between closely-related species.

3. *A genetically modified organism, or transgenic,* is the result of GE. Seventy percent of processed foods in American supermarkets now contain GMO ingredients.

4. High fructose corn syrup is a product derived from the corn kernel and extensively used in food processing, replacing natural sugar.

5. Recombinant Bovine Growth Hormone is a genetically engineered hormone injected into dairy cows to make them produce more milk. Many countries have banned its use.

6. Sustainability is the capacity to endure; biological systems remaining productive over time. Sustainability also means long-term maintenance of well-being of the natural world and the responsible use of all natural resources, including organic products.

7. Tertiary butyl hydroquinone is an antioxidant derived from petroleum, similar to butane. Approved in food processing at 0.02% concentration, one gram makes you sick (vomiting, nausea) and five grams will kill you.

8. Organic foods are foods produced without synthetic pesticides, artificial fertilizers, hormones, antibiotics, or genetic modification.

9. Giant processing facilities where 20 percent of the corn is processed into food and feed, soaked deconstructed, then reassembled as part of food processing.

10. Coarsely ground powder made from the cooked flesh of fish, primarily used in animal feed, especially for poultry, swine, mink, farm-raised fish, and pets.

11. A method of fishing involving one main line to which a series of shorter lines with baited hooks are attached. It is used at various depths to target different species, i.e., surface long lining for tuna or swordfish, bottom long lining for halibut or cod.

12. A fatty acid found in seafood and other sources. Recent research has found that these fatty acids can have a beneficial effect on the cardiovascular system as well as other aspects of human health.

13. This refers to seafood that has been frozen at its primary processor, and has not been slacked for reprocessing.

14. Opilio, the most common subspecies of Alaska snow crab, smaller and more bountiful than bairdi or tanner.

15. Any of seven species: blue fin tuna, albacore, yellow fin tuna, Southern blue fin tuna, big eye tuna, black fin tuna, and long tail tuna.

12 SUSHI ANSWERS

1. Tokyo and Osaka.
2. To avoid "sticky fingers."
3. Japanese horseradish; a green, knobby root that is ground.
4. It makes the rice fall apart and obliterates the taste of both rice and topping.
5. White, medium grain Japanese rice.
6. One to one and one-quarter.
7. Two to one to one third.
8. Three (seasoned, nonseasoned, and toasted).
9. Nori coated with vinegared rice *on the outside* and raw fish and/or vegetables placed inside.
10. "Inside-out" roll: avocado, cucumber, crab meat, toasted sesame seed, sushi rice, nori, mayonnaise (optional), and tobiko (optional).
11. Flying fish roe.
12. *Sushi:* made up of rice and vinegar, often accompany with fish and/or vegetables.
    Sashimi: thin slices of raw fish.
13. To cleanse the palate.
14. Hand roll, cone shaped; nori coated with vinegared rice, and raw fish and/or vegetables placed inside.
15. To avoid rice sticking to the mat, and it will also preserve the life of the mat.
16. To keep rice from sticking to fingers.

13 WOK ANSWERS

1. Cantonese and Szechuan
2. Iron woks
3. Water and nylon scouring pads
4. Twenty one
5. Chili, lemongrass, vinegar, garlic and salt
6. Master soy sauce
7. Both a and b
8. Szechuan pepper, native to the Szechuan province, the reddish-brown berries differ from peppers in that they grow on bushes instead of vines.
9. Cottonseed/canola blend
10. Water and cornstarch

14 CHEESE ANSWERS

1. What is curdling?
   A required step in cheese making is separating the milk into solid curds and liquid whey.
   Usually this is done by acidifying the milk and/or adding rennet.

2. True or false: Ultra pasteurized milk does not work with this recipe.
   True. The protein is being denatured by the high heat treatment of the process.

3. This aging period (also called ripening, or, from the French, *affinage*) is how long?
   A few days to several years

4. True or false: As a cheese ages, microbes and enzymes transform texture and intensify flavor.
   True. This transformation is largely a result of the breakdown of casein proteins.

5. What is rennet?
   A complex enzyme which is extracted from stomach of slaughtered young calves.

6. What function does rennet have in cheese making?
   It coagulates the milk to make the curd

7. What is the nutritional value of cheese?
   Cheese is a vital source of protein and calcium.
   It is the number one source of saturated fat.

8. The top cheese-producing country is:
   United States—30% of the world production

9. This country has the top per capita consumption of cheese:

Greece	68.4 pounds
France	57.4 pounds
Iceland	55.9 pounds
US	33 pounds, up from 11 pounds in 1970

10. Explain whey or milk serum.
    Whey is a co-product of cheese production. It separates from milk during curdling, when rennet or an edible acidic substance is added.

11. What effect does pasteurization have?
    It destroys unwanted bacteria in the milk and diminishes the nutrient value of the milk.

12. This is America's favorite cheese (one third of the annual per capita consumption):
    Mozzarella

15 CURE ANSWERS

1. We distinguish between *fresh, cooked,* and *dry* sausages, classification is subject to regional differences of opinion. Various metrics such as types of ingredients, consistency, and preparation are used.
2. Traditionally, sausage casings were made of the cleaned intestines. Today, however, natural casings are often replaced by collagen, cellulose, or even plastic casings.
3. Bacon that is only cured is also called fresh bacon. Fresh bacon may then be further dried for weeks or months in cold air, or it may be boiled or smoked.
4. This is a deboned chicken wrapped in its own skin along with ground meat and other ingredients, and then cooked. A galantine is cooked either by poaching it in stock or roasting it.
5. This is a deboned leg of a chicken, duck or other poultry stuffed with ground meat and other ingredients, tied and cooked. A ballotine is cooked by braising or poaching and can be served hot or cold.
6. Prague Powder No. 1, tinted cure, curing salt, and pink salt.
7. It prevents the growth of the deadly *Clostridium botulinum* bacteria, which causes botulism.
8. A combination of meat, fat, seasonings and other ingredients that are blended together through grinding or puréeing to form an emulsion.
9. A binder for forcemeat, panada consists of cubes of bread soaked in egg and milk.
10. A cured meat made from whole cuts of meat from hogs that are cured in salt or brine and then dry aged. The most famous of these is prosciutto; salumi is often confused with salami.

Testing Outlines

Objective

Following are the guidelines for testing culinary skills and knowledge. Each level of the culinary certification requires that the candidates be tested for skill proficiency equal to the level of certification at which they are or for which they are applying.

General Guidelines

- Our philosophy is to encourage growth from within. All culinary employees have the opportunity to be promoted within the department based on their demonstrated level of skills and knowledge, filling positions within the approved budget.
- Cooks will demonstrate proficiency for the level they are applying for.
- A written exam will be part two of the interview process, and a score of 80 percent is required to move to step three.
- A practical exam will be the third and final part of the interview process, and a score of 85 percent is required to pass the exam.

Training and Development

- Culinary team members will be certified for their level, new team members will be tested within ninety days.
- Team members will be notified at least fourteen days prior to the test and need to pass the written exam (one retake allowed) before qualifying for participation in the practical exam.
- The practical must be passed within thirty days to be confirmed in their current position. If, after the second attempt (initial test and one retest within sixty days), the individual still has not achieved a passing score, he or she will have to post for a lower position within the culinary department.

Culinary Certification Cook 1

An entry-level culinary team member responsible for preparing and cooking sauces, cold foods, fish, soups and stocks, meats, vegetables, eggs, and other food items; possesses a knowledge of food safety and sanitation and nutrition.

Written Exam Guidelines

- Complete all one hundred questions in sixty minutes.
- No support materials other than pencil and calculator are permitted.
- Eighty percent of items correctly answered represent a passing grade.

Recommended Texts

- *The Professional Chef, NRAEF ServSafe*, and handouts

Written Exam Question Makeup

Eighty questions: basic cooking
Twenty questions: sanitation

Practical Skill Proficiencies

Each level of culinary certification requires that the candidates be tested for skill proficiency equal to the level of certification for which they are applying.

Practical Exam Guidelines

- Candidates will be provided with all ingredients.
- Sanitation skills will be monitored at all times for compliance with standard rules.
- Sanitation infractions could lead to a failing grade.
- Professional uniform: all candidates must wear white chef's coat, hat, black pants, black shoes, and have apron, scarf, and side towel as well as name tag.
- Eighty-five points represent a passing grade.

Exam Time: 1.5 Hours

During the time allotted for your exam, prepare the following list of items; finish each according to industry standards and present final products to the examiners. As items are completed, you may present them at that time either by setting them on finished plates at the end of your work station or by approaching the examiner directly.

The candidate shall exhibit the following:

- Brunoise of onions, two ounces (may be cooked and used for the chicken preparation).
- Small dice of zucchini, four ounces (may be cooked and used for the preparation below).
- Fried parsley.
- Fabricate two servings of fried chicken tenders utilizing the standard breading procedure.
- Prepare and serve the chicken by applying appropriate seasoning and methodology and serve as main course with appropriate starch and vegetable (zucchini from above may be used).

Notes:

- Candidates should notify proctors ten minutes before they begin plating for final presentation.
- Appropriate organizational, safety, and sanitation skills greatly contribute to the candidate's success.

Culinary Certification Cook 2

An intermediate-level culinary team member responsible for preparing and cooking sauces, cold foods, fish, soups and stocks, meats, vegetables, eggs, and other food items; possesses a knowledge of food safety and sanitation and nutrition.

Written Exam Guidelines
- Complete all one hundred questions in sixty minutes.
- No support materials other than pencil and calculator are permitted
- Eighty percent of items correctly answered represent a passing grade.

Recommended Texts
- *The Professional Chef, NRAEF ServSafe*, and handouts

Written Exam Question Makeup
Eighty questions: basic cooking
Twenty questions: sanitation

Practical Skill Proficiencies
Each level of culinary certification requires that the candidates be tested for skill proficiency equal to the level of certification for which they are applying.

Practical Exam Guidelines
- Candidates will be provided with all ingredients.
- Sanitation skills will be monitored at all times for compliance with standard rules.
- Sanitation infractions could lead to a failing grade.
- Professional uniform: all candidates must wear white chef's coat, hat, black pants, black shoes, and have apron, scarf, and side towel as well as name tag.
- Eighty-five points represent a passing grade.

Exam Time: 2 Hours
During the time allotted for your exam, prepare the following list of items; finish each according to industry standards and present final products to the examiners. As items are completed, you may present them at that time either by setting them on finished plates at the end of your work station or by approaching the examiner directly.

The candidate shall exhibit the following:
- Julienne of carrot, two ounces.
- Batonet of carrot, four ounces (may also be cooked and used for the chicken preparation below).
- Finely chopped parsley, one-quarter cup (rinsed and readied for use)
- Standard *mirepoix*, one pound (may be used for chicken stock; reserve enough on a side plate to show the examiners as they grade your progress).
- Fabricate one whole chicken into:

  Two drumsticks, two thighs, and one wing, one chicken breast, first joint of the wing bone attached. It is clean. Skin is on. Cartilage and rib bones are removed.

  One skinless, boneless chicken breast. Tenderloin is removed.
- Prepare and begin to cook 1.5 gallons chicken stock (present the carcass to the examiner).
- Sauté one of the chicken breasts by applying appropriate seasoning and methodology, and serve as main course with appropriate starch and vegetable (batonet of carrots may be used).

Notes:
- Candidates should notify proctors ten minutes before they begin plating for final presentation.
- Appropriate organizational, safety, and sanitation skills greatly contribute to the candidate's success.

Culinary Certification Cook 3

An advanced level culinary team member responsible for preparing and cooking sauces, cold foods, fish, soups and stocks, meats, vegetables, eggs, and other food items; possesses a knowledge of food safety and sanitation and nutrition.

Written Exam Guidelines

- Complete all 120 questions in sixty minutes.
- No support materials other than pencil and calculator are permitted.
- Eighty percent of items correctly answered represent a passing grade.

Recommended Texts

- *The Professional Chef*, *NRAEF ServSafe*, and handouts

Written Exam Question Makeup

Ninety questions: basic cooking
Thirty questions: sanitation and nutrition

Practical Skill Proficiencies

Each level of PBC culinary certification requires that the candidates be tested for skill proficiency equal to the level of certification for which they are applying.

Practical Exam Guidelines

- Candidates will be provided with all ingredients.
- Sanitation skills will be monitored at all times for compliance with standard rules.
- Sanitation infractions could lead to a failing grade.
- Professional uniform: all candidates must wear white chef's coat, hat, black pants, black shoes, and have apron, scarf, and side towel as well as name tag.
- Eighty-five points represent a passing grade.

Exam Time: 2.5 Hours

During the time allotted for your exam, prepare the following list of items; finish each according to industry standards and present final products to the examiners. As items are completed, you may present them at that time either by setting them on finished plates at the end of your work station or by approaching the examiner directly.

The candidate shall exhibit the following:

Utilizing all the ingredients in this market basket, prepare a three-course menu, including an appetizer/salad and main course with appropriate accompaniments for each. Two portions of each course will be prepared and plated. Each ingredient must be used at least once.
You will be judged on utilization of the product provided; you may use additional starches, vegetables, and seasonings.

The three courses shall include:

- Appetizer/salad course as part of three-course meal.
- Main course (two or more accompanying vegetables and starch): approximately five to six ounces protein.
- Three classical vegetable cuts (i.e., julienne, brunoise, small dice, and paysanne).
- Three different cooking methods must be shown (i.e., broil, sauté, roast, boil, poach, steam, or grill).
- Appropriate vegetable and starch accompaniment for the main course (may use additional ingredients).
- Two different sauces using different methods (i.e., roux-based, reduction, or butter).

Notes:

- Candidate should notify proctors ten minutes before they begin plating for final presentation.
- Appropriate organization, safety and sanitation skills greatly contribute to the candidate's success.

Wild Rice Pancake
Yield: 10-12 pancakes

Ingredients:
1 cup all-purpose flour
1 tablespoon sugar
½ teaspoon baking powder
1 pinch salt
1 egg
½ cup buttermilk
2 cups wild rice, cooked
3 green onions, minced
3 tablespoons carrots, shredded
2 tablespoons cheddar cheese, shredded

Preparation:
1. In a large bowl, sift the dry ingredients together.
2. Add the egg and buttermilk. Stir together, but do not over mix.
3. Stir wild rice, green onions, carrots, and cheese into the batter.
4. Preheat nonstick pan on medium low.
5. Using a ½ cup measuring cup, pour mixture into heated nonstick pan.
6. After 2-3 minutes, turn the pancake over and cook for another 2-3 minutes.

Cranberry Compote Ingredients:
½ cup orange juice
1 cup sugar
3 cups cranberries, fresh or frozen
¼ cup maple syrup
Zest of 1 orange

Cranberry Compote Preparation:
1. In a medium saucepan, heat juice, sugar, cranberries, and orange zest.
2. Cover and bring to a slow boil. Simmer for 15–20 minutes.
3. Set aside for service.
4. Add more sugar or maple syrup if needed.

Local Sourcing
Central Indiana is the home of a hickory tree which produces "shagbark" syrup. Shagbark syrup is the result of a century-old process of extracting the syrup from shagbark harvested from the hickory trees. It's not made from sap like maple syrup; it's made from the bark of the tree. A shagbark tree sheds its bark when it becomes seven years old.
Hickory works produces about one thousand gallons of the thick, amber-colored syrup each year. Chefs and gourmet cooks prize the syrup for its complex, nutty flavor, which is very smoky and sweet at the same time.
"It is a really unique and special product. The history behind it is so interesting," says the only commercial producer in the country.

Epilogue

There is more to the Culinary Academy than the fifteen topics covered in this book, a full curriculum for stewards, and, last but not least, innovation at Level 3 classes.

A progressive training program to ensure food service safety, this HACCP/cook chill workshop is designed to share with the health department our "best practices," developed as part of our culinary academy. We invite local and state inspectors to spend a day in our facility observing our processes and get a hands-on experience with our chefs.

In the past, we always struggled with the turnover of inspectors and a fragmented inspection process. With this focused workshop, we implemented an educational platform where our chefs could have a constructive dialogue with inspectors and, side by side, learn from one another and build a professional relationship progressively.

The interactive seminar includes also a full HACCP review for our operation, including cheese making and curing meats. It provides insight to cook chill operation and is designed to foster collaboration with the inspectors, giving our chefs the opportunity to do what we do best, share our knowledge, and show leadership in the industry.

Continuous quality improvement is a cornerstone of our culture. To that end, we want to ensure that we are involving our chefs and managers in a way that is mutually beneficial.

We provide insight on industry trends and needs.
We keep the program relevant and growing.
We audit existing procedures and facilities.
We help make the program better and more innovative.
We are actively involved in the local community.
We provide opportunities for our graduating students.

On the Horizon for 2013 and Beyond

As the construction of the hotel project progresses, we are already fully immersed in concept development for the department, starting with a redefined and focused mission and vision.

Our Mission

"Deliver exceptional hospitality."

Our Vision

- We dominate the hospitality industry.
- We are the industry standard for culinary excellence.
- We have an outstanding reputation for exceptional service.
- We are the benchmark for attracting, developing, and retaining the most sought-after top talent in the hospitality industry.
- We are nationally recognized for our environmentally sound practices.
- We are trendsetters for creativity and innovation.
- We deliver a nationally recognized beverage program.

Values

Those are yet to be defined.

"Food culture has reminded us of the sacredness of food and the social importance of gathering together over meals. These ideals are the reason I became a cook, and I have been chasing them my whole career. But it's become obvious the restaurant is not the place to find them."

Willoughby Cooke wrote in *The New Inquiry* about the disconnect between sustainable food and sustainable employment practices in the restaurant business. He argues that the modern foodie may care more about the welfare of the chicken on the plate than the welfare of the person cooking it. It's a thought-provoking read.

"Science is the father of knowledge, but opinion breeds ignorance."

Hippocrates

17

RESOURCES

Cooking Ratios and Times for Selected Grains

Type	Ratio Grain: Liquid	Yield in Cups	Cooking Time in Minutes
Hominy Grits	1:4	3	25
Polenta	1:3	3–3½	35–45
Arborio Rice (Risotto)	1:3	3	20–30
Basmati Rice	1:1½	3	25
Converted Rice	1:1¾	4	25–30
Brown Rice	1:3	4	25
Wild Rice	1:3	4	30–45
Barley, Pearl	1:2	4	35–45
Buckwheat Groats (Kasha)	1:1½ to 2	2	15–20
Couscous	1:1½	2	12–15
Cracked Wheat	1:2	3	20

Approximate Soaking and Cooking Times for Dried Legumes

Type	Soaking Time in Hours	Cooking Time in Hours
Adzuki Beans	4	1
Black Beans	4	1½
Black-Eyed Peas	n/a	1
Chickpeas	4	2
Great Northern Beans	4	1
Lima Beans	4	1–1½
Pinto Beans	4	1–1½

Glossary

Accordion cut is a technique in butchery in which a thick piece of meat is extended into a thin one with a larger surface area. A series of parallel cuts are made from alternating sides of a roast almost all the way through, creating "hinges" which allow the meat to unfold into a long, flat, piece

Aioli is a tangy emulsified sauce similar to mayonnaise but made with olive oil instead of vegetable oil; garlic gives it punch.

Barding is a technique for cooking meats where the meat is wrapped in a layer of fat before cooking it. Pork fatback is commonly used for barding, although bacon is sometimes used for barding as well. Barding maintains the moisture of the meat while it cooks and helps keep it from overcooking.

Butter flying is a cutting technique; the piece of meat to be cut is laid out flat on a cutting board and cut in half parallel to the board from one side almost all the way to the other. A small "hinge" is left at the one side, which is used to fold the meat out like a book. The resemblance of this is what gives this cut its name.

Brunoise is a method of food preparation in which the food item is first cut into julienne and then turned 90° and cut again, producing cubes of a side length of 1/8 inch each side.

Chiffonade Is a knife technique used for cutting herbs and leaf vegetables such as lettuce into thin strips or ribbons.

Court bouillon is a flavored liquid for poaching fish and seafood, traditionally, court bouillon is water, salt, white wine, vegetable aromatics and flavored with *bouquet garni*

Cephalopod: a member of the group of mollusks that includes octopuses, squid, nautiluses and cuttlefishes. Cephalopods all have many arms and well-developed eyes.

Dashi Stock used in Japanese cooking is made from kelp and fermented bonito. It is the base for miso soup, clear broth, noodle broth, and many kinds of simmering liquid.

Demi-Glace is a rich, dark sauce made by combining half brown stock and half brown sauce (called Espagnole sauce) and then reducing that by half.

En papillote refers to a moist-heat cooking method where the food is enclosed in a packet of parchment paper or foil and then cooked in the oven.When cooking en papillote, there are usually some vegetables, herbs and seasonings included in the packet along with the main item. These additional ingredients, along with the main item, give off steam, which is what actually cooks the food. Therefore, en papillote cooking is basically a technique for cooking with steam.

Fish Oil Fatty oil from the bodies of fishes pressed from cooked fish during the manufacture of fishmeal and separated by centrifuge. Used in the manufacture of many products, such as margarine, cooking oil, cosmetics, caulking compounds, paints, industrial coatings, lubricants, water repellents, soaps, and candles.

Fishmeal Coarsely ground powder made from the cooked flesh of fish, primarily used in animal feed especially for poultry, swine, mink, farm-raised fish, and pets.

Glace de viand Is a thick syrup-like reduction of stock which is used to flavor other sauces. It is made from brown stock. Chicken glace, or glace de volaille, is made from chicken stock. Fish glace, or glace de poisson, is made from fish stock. Glaces are convenient because just a small spoonful can add a lot of flavor to a sauce or soup.

HFCS High-fructose corn syrup is a common sweetener that is used in soft drinks, breakfast cereals, cookies, snacks and many other processed foods. Like sucrose (table sugar), it is made up of a combination of the sugars fructose and glucose.

Humpy - Also known as "Pink" Salmon.

Ikura - Single-egg salmon caviar, generally from chum salmon or pink salmon, separated from the main egg skein, salted and sold in specialty markets. **J-Cut** - A method of removing pin bones and nape to produce a "table ready" product. J-Cut fillets are the premium trimmed fillets.

Julienne is a food preparation in which the item usually vegetables, is cut into 2"long thin strips with ¼" sides.

Larding Is a technique for cooking meats where long strips of fatback are woven through the meat using a needle called a larding needle. Larding maintains the moisture of the meat while it cooks and adds flavor.

Lardo di Colonnata Is cured lard the quarrymen who work Carrara marble have been using as sandwich meat for thousands of years.

Le Guide Culinaire Published by Auguste Escoffier, is still used as a major reference work, both in the form of a cookbook and a textbook on cooking.

Liaison Is a mixture of egg yolks and heavy cream that is used to thicken a sauce.

Long lining A method of fishing involving one main line to which a series of shorter lines with baited hooks are attached. Used at various depths to target different species, i.e. surface long lining for tuna or swordfish, bottom long lining for halibut or cod.

Lox Mild-cured salmon (soaked in brine for long periods, then soaked to remove the salt) that has been cold smoked.

Mirepoix Vegetable cut in ¾ inch cubes. The ratio is onions 50%, carrots 25% and celery 25%.

Matignon Is vegetable cut in cubes, the ratio is onions 1, carrots 2 and celery 1 and 1 part pork product (Ham or bacon). The size is determined by the intended use.

Molting The process by which a crustacean sheds its shell to accommodate growth.

Ocean Run Refers to salmon that are still in the ocean and are therefore bright and firm. "Ocean-Run" is also used by seafood companies to indicate a pack of random-weight or un sized products.

Omega-3 Fatty acids found in seafood and other sources. Recent research has found that these fatty acids can have a beneficial effect on the cardiovascular system as well as other aspects of human health.

Once Frozen Refers to seafood that has been frozen at its primary processor, and has not been slacked for reprocessing.

Opilio The most common subspecies of Alaska snow crab, smaller and more bountiful than bairdi.

PCBs Polychlorinated biphenyls are a group of chemicals that have been linked to cancer, interfere with the thyroid hormone and damage the neurological system. You can reduce your exposure by trimming fat from fish and meats before cooking them, avoiding fatty meats and dairy products, and limiting your intake of farmed salmon and catfish.

PUFI (Packed Under Federal Inspection) The seal that appears on products packed in accordance with the standards of this voluntary inspection program.

Purse Seining A method of fishing involving a long, deep net that stands like a fence in the water, supported at the surface by floats and held down by lead lines at the bottom. A fisherman in a skiff takes one end of the net around a school of fish and joins the seiner at the other end. The seiner then hauls in the wire or rope purse line strung through the bottom of the net forming a "purse" to capture the fish.

RBGH Recombinant Bovine Growth Hormone is a genetically engineered hormone injected into dairy cows to make them produce more milk. Many countries have banned its use.

Remouillage Is a second stock made from the same set of bones.

Roux Is a mixture of butter and flour, cooked until bubbly. A brown roux can be used as the basis for etouffee and brown sauce. If not browned at all, it is the base of béchamel, velouté, or white sauce.

Secondary Processor Refers to a processing facility that utilizes previously frozen seafood and further processes it (into specialty cut, batter/bread, etc.) before selling.

Small goods Is a term used in Australia to refer to small meat products such as sausage or bacon.

Smolt A young salmon ready to live in salt water.

Snap 'N Eats Crab legs that have been cooked, frozen, and scored through the shell so they can be hand cracked for easy eating.

Stevia Is a native to regions from the Americas, commonly known as *sweet leaf*, *sugar leaf*, or simply *stevia*, is widely grown for its sweet leaves. As a sweetener and sugar substitute its taste has a slower onset and longer duration than that of sugar although some of its extracts may have a bitter or licorice-like aftertaste at high concentrations. It has up to 300 times the sweetness of sugar.

Trans fat free Trans fats do exist in nature but also occur during the processing of polyunsaturated fatty acids in food production. The consumption of trans fats increases the risk of coronary heart disease by raising levels of LDL cholesterol and lowering levels of "good" HDL cholesterol.

Trailer Leg - In snow crab, also called the fifth leg.

Trolling A fishing method in which lines with lures or baits are towed behind a boat. It is particularly important in the harvesting of Salmon.

Tobiko Is the Japanese word for the flying fish roe, widely known for its use in sushi dishes.

Tuna Any of seven species: blue fin tuna, albacore, yellow fin tuna, Southern blue fin tuna, big eye tuna, black fin tuna, and long tail tuna.

V-Cut A method of removing pin bones by making a V-shaped cut along both sides of the pin bone strip, leaving most of the nape.

Umami Is one of the five basic tastes, together with sweet, sour, bitter and salty. Umami is described as a savory or meaty taste. It can be tasted in cheese and soy sauce, and in many other fermented and aged foods, this taste is also present in tomatoes, grains, and beans.

Vin Santo Or holy wine is a style of Italian dessert wine, in Tuscany; these wines are often made from white grape varieties such as Trebbiano and Malvasia

Sources
Food in History, Reay Tannahill, 1973
Hering's Dictionary of Classical and Modern Cookery, Richard Hering, 1976
Le Repertoire De La Cuisine, Louis Saulnier, 1977
Cheese Making, Ricki Carrol, 2002
Complete Book of Pork Bruce, Aidell 2004
The Professional Chef, Eighth Edition, CIA, 2006
The Story of Sushi, Trevor Corson, 2008
Charcuterie, Fritz Sonnenschmidt, CMC, Delmar Cengage Learning, 2009
The End of Char Kway Teow, Dr. Leslie Tay, 2011

Internet
www.academiabarilla.com/
www.acfchefs.org/
www.eatwisconsincheese.com/
www.eatwellguide.com
www.foodincmovie.com/index.php
www.growingpower.org
www.hotelfandb.com
www.michaelpollan.com
www.montereybayaquarium.org
www.nraef.org
www.sustainabletable.com
www.scrubclub.org/assets/pdf/handango.pdf
http://truefoodnow.org/
www.wacs2000.org/wacs2009_beta/en/home/index.php
http://en.wikipedia.org/wiki/Category:French_chefs
http://en.wikipedia.org/wiki/List_of_chefs_(antiquity_to_the_20th_century)

Culinary Schools
www.bocusedorusa.org/about.html#mission
www.ciaprochef.com/
www.cornell.edu
www.steigenberger-akademie.de/
www.gentingstaracademy.com/
www.icif.com/
www.jwu.edu

All photography provided by the author unless otherwise stated
Shepherd Express Cover used with the permission of Shepherd Express magazine
Page 109-Food is a weapon from UNT Libraries Government Documents Department

Page 9, Culinary Academy Schedule
Page 160, Chef Gebauer pulling mozzarella cheese
Page 207, Faculty chefs Robert Dietiker, Peter Gebauer, Tony Ho, Steve Johnson and Mike Nagovan
Used with the permission of the Forest County Potawatomi Community Wisconsin, Potawatomi Hotel Casino. ©2013 Forest County Potawatomi Community Wisconsin. All rights reserved.

"Do not always follow on the path laid down. It leads where others have already gone."

Alexander Graham Bell

18

PREVIEW
Street Food and Spare Parts
(Currently in the making)

The History of Street Food

Street food is ready-to-eat food or drink sold in a street or other public place, such as a market or fair, by a hawker or vendor, often from a cart or portable stall. While some street foods are regional, many are not, having spread beyond their region of origin. Most street foods are also classed as both finger food and fast food, and are cheaper on average than restaurant meals. According to a 2007 study from the Food and Agriculture Organization, 2.5 billion people eat street food every day.

Evidence of a large number of street food vendors was discovered during the excavation of Pompeii. Street food was widely utilized by poor urban residents of ancient Rome, whose tenement homes did not have ovens or hearths, with chickpea soup being one of the common meals, along with bread and grain paste.
A traveling Florentine reported in the late 1300s that in Cairo, people carried picnic cloths made of rawhide to spread on the streets and eat their meals of lamb kebabs, rice, and fritters that they had purchased from street vendors. In Renaissance Turkey, many crossroads saw vendors selling "fragrant bites of hot meat," including chicken and lamb that had been spit roasted.

In ancient China, where street foods generally catered to the poor, wealthy residents would send servants to buy street foods and bring meals back for their masters to eat in their homes. Sushi during the Edo period quickly became a popular street food in Japan during that time.

Aztec marketplaces had vendors that sold beverages such as *atolli* (a gruel made from maize dough), almost fifty types of tamales (with ingredients that ranged from the meat of turkey, rabbit, gopher, frog, and fish to fruits, eggs, and maize flowers), as well as insects and stews. After Spanish colonization of Peru and importation of European food stocks such as wheat, sugarcane, and livestock, most commoners continued primarily to eat their traditional diets, but did add grilled beef hearts sold by street vendors.

During the American colonial period, street vendors in Philadelphia sold "pepper pot soup" which included tripe, "oysters, roasted corn ears, fruit, and sweets," with oysters being a low-priced commodity until the 1910s when overfishing caused prices to rise. As of 1707, after previous restrictions that had limited their operating hours, street food vendors had been banned in New York City. Many women of African descent made their living selling street foods in America in the eighteenth and nineteenth centuries; with products ranging from fruit, cakes, and nuts in Savannah to coffee, biscuits, pralines, and other sweets in New Orleans.

Peru and the Andes

Peru is a country that holds not just a variety of ethnic mixes since times ranging from the Inca Empire to the Viceroyalty and the Republic, but also a climatic variety. The mixing of cultures and the variety of climates differ from city to city, so geography, climate, culture, and ethnic mix determine the variety of local cuisine. When I wrote *Omnivore's Travel* I briefly touched on the region's food as I traveled from La Paz through Bolivia to Cuzco and Lima by way of Lake Titicaca and the ruins of Macchu Picchu. While maize is a staple in the lower regions, the population in the Andes above an elevation of ten thousand feet relied on potatoes and quinoa. The Incas in their times "freeze dried" potatoes, and today the same process is still widely used in the fabrication of "chuna."

In the valleys and plains of the Andes, the locals' diet is still based on corn (maize), potatoes, and an assortment of tubers, as it has been for hundreds of years. Meat comes from indigenous animals like alpacas and guinea pigs, but also from imported livestock like sheep and swine. As with many rural cultures, most of the more elaborate dishes were reserved for festivities, while daily meals were simple affairs. Nowadays, festive dishes are consumed every day, though they tend to be on the heavy side and demand a large appetite.

Andean cooking's main freshwater fish is the trout, raised in fisheries in the region.

Where there are historical immigrant Chinese populations, the style of food has evolved and been adapted to local tastes and ingredients, and modified by the local cuisine, to greater or lesser extents. This has resulted in a number of forms of fusion cuisine, often very popular in the country in question, and some of these, such as ramen (Japanese/Chinese), have become popular internationally.

Yellow Causa with Lump Crab
Yield: 8 servings

Aioli Ingredients:
1 whole egg
2 teaspoons Key lime juice
1 cup extra virgin olive oil
10 black olives, pitted
1 pound lump crab
1 avocado
1 large tomato, diced
1 bunch cilantro

Ingredients:
2 large yellow potatoes
¼ cup extra virgin olive oil
1 Key lime, juiced
1 tablespoon Ají Amarillo paste
To taste: salt and white pepper

Preparation:
1. Combine the egg, salt, and Key lime juice in a blender or food processor. Blend for 1 minute on a low speed.
2. With the motor running, add the olive oil in a slow, steady stream to form a thick mayonnaise. When all of the oil is incorporated, shut off the motor and scrape down the sides of the jar with a spatula.
3. Empty the aioli into a bowl, leaving just enough in the bottom of the blender to cover the blades.
4. Add the pitted olives and blend for a few more minutes to form a smooth purée.
5. Add the olive purée to the reserved aioli and mix thoroughly until the mixture is uniform in color and consistency, then refrigerate.
6. Scrub the potatoes and place them in a large pot with plenty of salted water. Bring to a boil And cook until tender, about 10 minutes.
7. Strain the potatoes well, and when they are cool enough to handle (but still warm), peel and Mash them finely by pressing them through a fine mesh sieve or a ricer.
8. Add the olive oil, Key lime juice, ají Amarillo paste, and salt. Mix thoroughly until all the ingredients are well incorporated.
9. Lightly oil and line individual cup molds with plastic wrap. Line the base of the mold with a layer of the potato mixture, pressing down lightly and leveling it with the back of a spoon.
10. Add a layer of the crab and then another layer of the potato.
11. Next add a layer of sliced avocado, sprinkled with a little lime juice and salt.
12. Finish off with a layer of the potato mixture and chill for at least 1 hour until ready to use.
13. Garnish with the aioli, diced tomato, and cilantro.

DID YOU KNOW?

Ají Amarillo is an important ingredient for Peruvian and Bolivian cooking and serves as a condiment in many dishes and sauces. In Peru, the chilis are mostly used fresh. In Bolivia, they are dried and ground.

ABOUT THE AUTHOR

Chef Gebauer is a seasoned professional with over forty years of experience in the hospitality industry, opening new resorts, cruise lines and developing food & beverage concepts.

During his professional career Chef Gebauer has been involved in consulting projects around the world, earned many memberships and awards. He catered to royal families, presidents and governments, and was featured on TV shows in Germany as well as the US. He cooked at the James Beard House in New York City and frequently at the Grand Old Opry, Nashville.

Growing up at the foothills of the Bavarian Alps he had a humble childhood in the country side. Beginning his culinary career with a traditional apprenticeship in a boutique hotel he became certified chef with honor after three years. Then he sailed around the world onboard luxury cruise lines, taking on his first sous chef position with Peninsula in Hong Kong, the Middle East would follow before he returned to Germany becoming Certified Master Chef. Shortly after that he was appointed Executive Chef onboard the legendary SS Norway at age thirty. After a few years he found a new challenge with the startup for both Star Cruises in Singapore and later Disney Cruise Line in Florida. Opening the Aventura Spa Palace in Cancun followed before he accepted a position at the Gaylord Opryland Resort in Nashville.

In 2006 he became the Executive Chef at Potawatomi Bingo Casino, the largest Native American Casino operation without a hotel. His department has been recognized for its accomplishments in food safety as a finalist at the 2013 NRA Shows Operators Innovation Awards in Chicago.

He is a member of the American Culinary Federation and is an advisor to several culinary schools in the Milwaukee area as well as the Wisconsin Restaurant Association board. He is actively supporting the community and local area charities, and contributes frequently to the Hotel F&B Magazine, a National industry publication.

Chef Peter now lives in Germantown and enjoys family time with his wife Aime, son Daniel and daughter Anna Claudia; together they also practice Tae Kwon Do.

Chef published his first book in 2009, Omnivore's Travel takes an unprecedented approach in examining his international career, a smorgasbord of bizarre food experiences and provocative cultural history, this book provides insight on the current challenges and trends in our industry for the reader. Part in-depth reference, part career guide, it is entertainment for travelers, foodies and peers alike.

42051151R00141

Made in the USA
Lexington, KY
08 June 2015